THE PIG AND PASTRY COOKBOOK

STEVE HOLDING

Photography by Karen Turner

 Pig Publishing

Special thanks to Graham and Nicki Law for all their support and advice.

Most importantly, to all the boys and girls, past and present who have worked at The Pig. You've had to be coffee makers, salad creators, milkshake mixers, washer-uppers, order takers, tidy-er-uppers, cake makers, veg peelers and much more. You've coped with the queues and the long days and you've done it all with a smile on your face. Thank you.

Text © Steve Holding, 2015
Photography © Karen Turner, 2015
Design and Layout © Alexandra Vintila, 2015

Photographer Karen Turner
Designer Alexandra Vintila
Editor Justine Brooks

First published in 2015 by Pig Publishing
35 Bishopthorpe Road
York
YO23 1NA

Reprinted 2016
Printed and bound by Elle Media Group

10 9 8 7 6 5 4 3 2 1

A catalogue record for this book is
available from the British Library.

ISBN: 978-0-9933883-0-9

All profits from the sale of this book will be donated to Candlelighters

Registered Charity No: 1045077

"To all children affected by cancer.
You are braver than you will ever know"

"To Karen, Alex and Justine.
Who provided their skills for free and devoted
their time to create this book for a charity close to
our hearts. Thank you"

CONTENTS

Rosette Awards

AA

Something, Something
Culinary Excellence
2015

Michelin Star Award

~~Tang Hall~~ Eton 1979

Pig & Pate's
Lowcut
Andied C. £150
£100
£100

STEPHEN REDMAN

Candlelighters Chair of Trustees

For that most excellent establishment "The Pig and Pastry"

No one expects a visit from childhood cancer until it knocks on your door.

When it does, the patterns of life go out the window and the impact on families is beyond belief.

How do you carry on, what do you do, when each day is like an avalanche hanging over you that could swamp you at any minute?

Candlelighters is a Yorkshire charity that has been standing with families for over 40 years and supporting them in their time of need, supporting the NHS in their delivery of treatment and supporting the fight against cancer in the laboratory with cutting edge research.

In fact Candlelighters is the only charity you can support that helps every family in the region that is fighting childhood cancer and our research programme helps the worldwide fight against the disease.

Steve Holding has put together some of his wonderful recipes and award winning photographer Karen Turner has photographed them, creating an excellent book to help in this fight. The Pig and Pastry has an amazing reputation, and their book will only enhance that.

Please enjoy their food, enjoy the ideas in this book that will excite your taste buds and whilst you are doing this remember that by buying this book you are helping families face the greatest trial of their lives.
Thank you for buying this book, and thank you for supporting Candlelighters!

STEVE HOLDING

Chef

For me, The Pig and Pastry isn't just about the food. I know, this is a cookbook. But look at the café from my perspective (peering out from the kitchen): I don't see people coming in just to eat, the food is secondary to why you lovely people are here. It's not often that I get the opportunity, and when I do, I get a real kick out of just stopping to look out into the café and taking it all in. It's busy, it's loud, there's banter between the staff and customers, there's an energy. People are chatting and laughing, enjoying each other's company. People are sharing tables and striking up conversations with strangers.

One of my favourite things is when I see someone who has been stuck in the queue for a while place their order and look for somewhere to sit. Perhaps they'll look a little grumpy, reluctantly ask other guests if the empty seat at their table is free and sit down. 'Damn, this guy's not happy about sharing' I think to myself, but then moments later I'll see the whole table chatting and joking with each other.

When we opened we had in mind that the big table in the window would be a sharing table. It was a gamble really - I'd seen it in a café where I used to stop off for a coffee on my way to work in London and really liked the idea. What I didn't expect was that customers would also start sharing the little tables (don't ever come here on a first date). I now know that some friendships have been made in The Pig - I was once invited to a customer's party, there were lots of other customers there too and when I chatted to them I was surprised to find out that most of them only knew each other because of the café: I'd always thought that many of them had already been friends.

Back in 2008, Julia was still a children's nurse and I was happy as a chef out in the country where we'd just won Yorkshire Life Pub Restaurant of the Year. Then our good friends Nicki and Graham told us about the 'empty shop round the corner'. We started to think about opening a restaurant, did our research, did some sums, talked ourselves out of it, put the idea aside. Then on a trip to London we fell in love with a couple of deli/cafés. So we came back, did our sums again and then got excited about opening our own deli/café. It was at the time of the financial crisis, so the excitement and giddiness was soon replaced by worry and night tremors. Banks and well established companies were folding and everyday on the news, the story of the economy was bleak. Some friends told us that it wouldn't work, not because the economy was terrible, but because the neighbourhood was just the wrong location. Well, we carried on and opened regardless and sometimes it's just oh-so sweet to prove people wrong.

In the summer of 2012, our little girl was taken ill, and was diagnosed with a serious brain tumour. A number of operations, intensive radiotherapy and almost a year of chemotherapy followed for Ruby at Leeds General

Infirmary and St. James Hospital in Leeds. For me, the first few weeks of that summer are a hazy blur, but we'll never forget the generosity and compassion of customers, staff and friends at that time. People offered to wash up at the café (even though they were terrible at it!), they drove us to Leeds, brought in audiobooks and fun tactile games (Ruby completely lost her sight as a result of the tumour), and showed their support by organising fundraisers for the charities helping Ruby. All the letters and cards of support made a difference too. I always knew we lived in a lovely area, but I never really understood the great sense of community that we have here until that summer of 2012 when so many people (some I had never even met before) went out of their way to do something nice.

Candlelighters

Being in hospital as a child can be terrifying and stressful and spending long periods on a ward can be tedious and deflate a child's spirit. Candlelighters is a charity that really helps keep the kids distracted from the day to day worries. When you have lost your sight or are unable to get out of bed, it's not easy to rely on the usual fun stuff anymore. The Candlelighters team at LGI and St. James were amazing at helping Ruby find fun things to do.

The charity buys specialist medical equipment with the funds raised, provides enthusiastic staff who are great with the kids and parents, supplies the wards with games, toys, entertainment and crafts and creates family areas within the wards to help make a space for some family normality. I'm not doing them justice here, I know they do much more as well. As a family, we are hugely grateful to the difference they made to our lives during Ruby's time in hospital.

Karen Turner. Photographer

This book wouldn't be here at all if wasn't for Karen, the maniac with the camera. Not only was it her idea, but she's the one with the big stick and without her prodding me with this stick (sometimes whacking me with it) I'd still be 'getting round to it'. More than just the photographer, Karen has pretty much coordinated the whole project (partly because she is a complete control freak and partly because she's bloody good at it). With the exception of a couple of shoots we did in the flat above the shop (with the laundry hanging up in the background!) Karen has had to do all the photography, dancing around us in a normal busy work day environment. No food stylists, no special lighting and no phony staged shots. Oh, one more thing, she has done all of this for free. Thanks you.

Alexandra Vintila. Designer

It turns out that you don't just need awesome pictures and some badly written recipes to make a cookbook. You also need a great designer. A great designer who will do it for free! Not easy to find, but we have been really lucky to find Alex who has squeezed this book in between her real job and busy life. Thank you Alex!

Justine Brooks. Editor

What the heck? It also turns out that you need an editor to help make a book too. Justine gave up her valuable time at the last minute to help us bring it all together with her stacks of knowledge and experience. Thank you Justine.

KAREN TURNER

Photographer

I discovered The Pig and Pastry by accident 6 years ago (it's tucked away in an area of York that I wouldn't normally visit) but when I did I soon became a 'regular' even though I live near Leeds.

In 2012 I went through a tough time in my personal life, and had a long gap where I couldn't visit the café as it held a lot of associated memories for me. When I eventually plucked up the courage to return, the lovely staff asked after me, and noticed that I hadn't been in for a long while. A sense of belonging is important to us all (even more so when you are going through a difficult time) and although I didn't live in the area, they made me feel like I had a place there and I had been missed - it meant an awful lot.

The following year I noticed that there were a lot of charity events happening in the café and I learned of Ruby's illness, so I offered to give some family portrait gift vouchers as raffle prizes when the family were fund-raising for Candlelighters. This was the first time I had heard of the charity, and being an ex nurse and a children's photographer, it struck a chord with me.

When I was capturing the prize winners' children and grandchildren, I learnt a lot more about Steve and Julia, the café and Bishopthorpe Road. What came across most strongly was the loyalty of the winners to the family, many of whom bought raffle tickets over and over again, not wanting to win anything, just wanting to show their support for Ruby.

The cookbook idea was born one day when I overheard a customer listing some ingredients he had bought to Steve, and asking him what could he make with them for dinner that night ... It was then that it dawned on me how much Steve's knowledge was valued, and how a cookbook could be a fantastic way to raise funds, at the same time giving every person who contributed a lovely book, all about their favourite neighbourhood café and food.

The cookbook was a long time in the persuading ... and only really seemed to feel like it could become a reality when we found Alex, our designer. Her creative use of fonts, illustrations and image layouts got both Steve and I really excited and started the ball rolling properly.

The first couple of shoots were in the storeroom above the café. There was very little light and the cookers were in the darkest corner of the room. So Steve dragged a freezer to the small window and put a two-ring hob on top of it so we could bring natural light into the shoot. I fretted big-style.

I had spent so long convincing Steve that we could do this, and suddenly worried whether I would be able to get any technically great images from a camping style cooker perched on a chest freezer. How wrong I was. We were able to get amazing results and I knew we were onto a winner as soon as I saw the first photographs!

Fifteen shoots, hundreds of emails, umpteen lists and a tonne of hard work from us all later, I met Justine from Fly Media. She came on board when I was finding it hard to believe that we could have the book ready for autumn. The images were all there, recipes written, proofreading started, but bringing it all together was causing me to lose sleep. Her editing skills, and deadline management were just what we needed, and I am so grateful that she has helped us.

As a result of working on this amazing book, the images I captured have changed my business in a way I never dreamed possible, elevating my real food photography, and winning me a finalist prize in a very prestigious international food photography competition.

High praise and reward indeed. However the main reward for me is personal rather than business. Being able to help the fantastic charity that supported Ruby and her family when they needed it most; making some great friends and feeling even more a part of this lovely community are the icing on the cake!

"Glorified..."
Says highly qualified TripAdvisor reviewer
"Not bad"
Tracey, London
"Do you do Jacket Potatoes?"
Margaret, York
SELECTED POTATOES
SELECTED POTATOES
SELECTED

ALEXANDRA VINTILÃ

Designer

When people ask me what my contribution to this project is, I find myself simply saying "I designed the cookbook". However this in no way expresses the part I have played and how I feel about being involved with this book. Graphic design is one of my favourite things in the world, the idea of expressing your thoughts on a blank canvas where anything can happen truly excites me. The Pig and Pastry cookbook has given me a massive opportunity to do what I love doing and build success along the way. When I started working on this project I was working as a part-time designer, with no experience and no involvement with complex projects. However the challenge that was put in front of me gave me the confidence and understanding to create bigger and better opportunities for myself. For this I have to thank Karen and Steve, they showed faith in me to design the book and I have loved every minute of working together. The whole project has been a fantastic collaboration that has ended up with the production of something very special and unique.

Steve's recipes are truly amazing. Having sampled the food and spent time in the café myself I can totally understand the success of The Pig and Pastry. Steve's sense of humour and personality is written all over the book and he should be extremely proud of what he has created. Karen has not only taken some beautiful photography to bring the recipes inside the book to life, she has also masterfully managed the project from start to finish. She has kept us motivated and enthusiastic throughout this process.

At the beginning the whole project seemed daunting and the idea of completing a whole cookbook was something I never thought I was capable of. However now I can honestly say it has been one of the most exciting and gratifying experiences in my career so far.

BREAKFAST

Free
Sausage !

KIPPERS & BROWN BREAD

People worry about the whiff, the head on, the bones and they sound way too unfashionable to order, but they're a breakfast classic. Full of essential oils and they taste delicious.
We get our Kippers from the excellent smoker Justin Staal, who smokes the herrings over apple & oak wood chippings from his farm in Long Riston, East Yorkshire. We used to serve whole kippers with the heads on, they look spectacular, but people seem to prefer their breakfasts without heads. Weird.

Serves 1

1 kipper –pair of fillets whole
1 ripe tomato
25g butter
freshly chopped parsley
wedge of lemon
brown bread & butter

Preparation

Pre heat the grill or oven to 200 C.
Heat a large non stick or heavy iron pan. Get it quite hot, add a splash of oil then carefully place the kipper fillets in flesh side down. Turn the heat down a little.
Season the tomatoes and add to the pan.
Once the kippers are browned on the flesh side, flip them over and finish the cooking under the grill or in the oven. Turn out onto the plate and carefully drain away any oil in the pan. Place the pan back on a low heat and add the butter until melted and frothy. Pour over the kippers and tomatoes, Finish with freshly chopped parsley and a wedge o' lemon.

Brown Bread

250g strong white flour	7g yeast
200g granary or wholemeal flour	225g water
10g salt	100g poolish (50g wholemeal flour, 50g water plus a pinch of yeast)
5g sugar	

The night before, mix together your poolish and cover. Allow to ferment over night.

Put the yeast, sugar and water together in a bowl and set aside while you weigh out the dry ingredients.

Weigh out the flour & salt, then mix into the water, add the poolish and knead for several minutes on a floured worktop.

Once you're happy it's smooth and elastic, cover and leave to prove.

Turn out onto a floured top, dimple and fold and shape into a fat cylinder.

Pre heat oven to 210 C.

Place into a lightly oiled 800g bread tin, cover and leave until doubled in size.

Bake in the centre of the oven for 25 - 30 mins.

Leave to cool for a couple of hours before attempting to slice. Slicing into hot bread ruins the structure of the crumb, leaving you with a soggy heavy loaf.

HEUVOS A LA FLAMENÇA (GYPSY EGGS!)

The first part of this recipe is a hearty, spicy supper dish on its own, great with crispy duck confit or slow roast strips of pork belly. But add eggs into the equation with some crusty bread for dunkin' and it becomes an amazing breakfast/brunch dish.

Serves 4 hearty portions

8 eggs

1 onion

2 cloves of garlic

2 chorizo sausages (about 140g)

400g tin of butterbeans

400g tin of tomatoes

4 rashers of streaky bacon

2 red peppers

bay leaf

few sprigs of thyme

1 tsp smoked paprika

100g frozen peas

50g parsley

a little chicken stock

Bread for dunkin'

Preparation

In a casserole pan, start to sweat the sliced onions down in a little olive oil over a medium heat until the onions have really softened, but have not coloured too much.

Add the crushed garlic and smoked paprika, roughly chopped bacon and then the sliced chorizo sausages.

Add the tomatoes, butterbeans, bay leaf, thyme and enough stock to just cover everything. Simmer for an hour.

Lastly, stir in the peas and take off the heat for now.

Crack your eggs into a large ovenproof dish and season them.

Carefully ladle the butterbean stew over the eggs, careful not to break the yolks and place into the oven for 20 -25 minutes (or until the whites are set and the yolks are still runny).

Remove from the oven, drizzle with a little olive oil and sprinkle with chopped parsley.

Serve with good crusty bread on the side.

SOFT BIG BAPS

We tried numerous recipes to create a soft floury bap and we really struggled to get it right. Until one day, I mentioned it to Steve, our flour guy and annoyingly he knew the answer straight away ... "lower your temperature and increase your fats". Thanks! Lo and behold, soft, floury baps.

Makes 12

875g strong white flour
15g salt
15g sugar
10g yeast or 7g dried yeast
75ml veg oil
550g water

Preparation

Set the oven to 175 C (this is low for bread baking).
Lightly flour a 30mm by 42mm tray.
Stir the yeast into the water and add the oil.
Mix all the dry ingredients together and then add all the liquid. Mix and knead for a good 7 to 10 mins.
Rest, cover and leave to prove for 30 - 40 mins.
Knock back and divide into 12 x 120g lumps.
Roll into tight balls of dough and sit them in the tray, evenly spaced out.
Dust with flour, cover and leave to prove (just over double in size).
Into the oven, gently. Bake for 12 minutes, spin around, then 12 minutes more.
Onto a cooling rack and leave to cool before eating.

CHORIZO & SCRAMBLED EGGS

{ We use a special type of chorizo for this breakfast dish. It's a 'parilla' chorizo sausage which is not as firm as the 'horse shoe' ring chorizo sausage that you can get in some delicatessens. This sausage is only semi cured and not made to be eaten raw, but grilled or added to stews and is oh, so juicy! }

Serves 4

6 Brindisa parilla dulce chorizo
sausages
8 eggs
8 tbsp double cream

50g butter
8 slices of sourdough
chopped parsley

Preparation

De-string and cut the chorizo sausages into thick slices - about 1cm thick rounds.

Set into a pan with no oil over a medium heat. Plenty of oil and juice will come out of the sausage slices as they cook.

Stir often until they are just cooked and set aside.

Start the eggs …

On a low heat, add the butter. When melted, add the eggs and break up in the pan with your wooden spoon (a metal spoon will ruin your non stick pan).

Continue stirring your eggs on a low heat. It may seem like not a lot's happening, but don't be tempted to turn up the heat, you could end up with a pan full of omelette chunks instead of smooth, creamy eggs.

As the eggs are almost cooked (they should be coming together, but still slightly runny), take off the heat and stir in a twist of pepper and the cream. The residual heat in the pan should be enough to finish them off with a little more stirring. If not, back on the stove, low heat and stir until they are to your liking.

Spoon the eggs over the toasted sourdough, and top the eggs with the chorizo pieces. Drizzle some of the chorizo juice over the eggs and sausage and finish with some chopped parsley.

FIVE SEED BREAD

{ This is the one loaf we like to make the day before. It's not a sourdough, but the long ferment gives it a great taste and a killer crust. If you don't like the taste of fennel or aniseed, then leave out the fennel seeds. This is our most popular loaf, but occasionally, someone will say "what was that weird seed?". It's by far the strongest taste in the loaf, but I think it tastes great and it smells incredible when it's toasting. }

Makes 2 x 450g loaves (or 1 big loaf)

250g strong white flour
250g granary flour
10g fresh or 7g dried yeast
10g salt
10g sugar
370g water

2 tbsp pumpkin seeds
2 tbsp poppy seeds
2 tbsp sesame seeds
2 tbsp sunflower seeds
1 tbsp fennel seeds

Preparation

Set the yeast and sugar working in the water.

Meanwhile, weigh the rest of the ingredients into the bowl of a free standing mixer. When the water starts to look nice and frothy, add to the bowl and mix for a good 10 minutes.

Cover the bowl with cling film or a tea towel and leave to prove until doubled in size.

Pre heat the oven to 240 C.

Remove the dough from the bowl and turn out onto a floured worktop. Try and create some tension in the loaf by stretching and folding the loaf a couple of times (this will help the loaf stand up proud!) and then rolling into a tight roll. Place into a lightly oiled tin, lightly dust with flour and loosely cover with a cloth.

Leave to prove until doubled in size. Bake in the centre of the oven, lightly mist with water (if you have a water spray trigger bottle): this will help the loaf get a good crust.

Bake at 240 C for 25 mins, turn out onto a cooling rack and leave to cool for a good hour before eating.

SMOKED SALMON & SCRAMBLED EGGS

{ I think a good non-stick sauce pan and a wooden spoon are key to good scrambled eggs. Ever used a regular saucepan to scramble eggs and wondered why you end up with a small portion? Most of the egg ends up sticking to the side of the pan.

I always season eggs, but with this recipe, I leave out the salt. The smoked salmon, which is naturally salty, seasons the eggs. All you'll need is a little black pepper. }

Serves 4

300g sliced smoked salmon
8 eggs
8 tbsp double cream
50g of butter

chopped chives
freshly ground black pepper
4 thick slices of buttered Five
Seeded toast (previous recipe)

Preparation

On a low heat, add the butter. When melted, add the eggs and break up in the pan with a wooden spoon (a metal spoon will ruin your non stick pan).

Continue stirring your eggs on a low heat. It may seem like not a lot is happening, but don't be tempted to turn up the heat: you could end up with a pan full of omelette chunks instead of smooth, creamy eggs.

As the eggs are almost cooked (they should be coming together, but still slightly runny), take off the heat and stir in the chives a twist of pepper, smoked salmon and the cream. The residual heat in the pan should be enough to finish them off with a little more stirring. If not, back on the stove, low heat and stir until they are to your liking.

Serve over hot buttered toast!

SHAKSHUKA

We treat this dish like a veggie version of the Gypsy Eggs. I've seen a number of recipes for Shakshuka and they all seem to vary - including the spelling! I worked with a Moroccan guy in London who loved this dish, only without the eggs. He preferred it served like a little stew to go with grilled fish. When he gave me the recipe, it had absolutely no quantities:

"How much paprika Issam?"
"Not much"
"Are tomatoes the main ingredient?"
"Not really"
"Ok, you make it, I'll watch!"

I took note of the quantities. But watching him make the dish, he never really weighed anything out. He was literally tipping spices out of the tub into the pan. Anyway, the results were brilliant and this is more or less it (but with eggs, not fish).

Serves 4 (maybe more!)

8 eggs
1 large onion - sliced
3 large peppers - sliced
2 x 400g tins of tomatoes
1 tsp ground cumin
1 tsp smoked paprika
1/2 tsp ground coriander
pinch of saffron

100mls olive oil
6 cloves garlic
1 large bay leaf and some sprigs of thyme tied up together
200mls vegetable stock
50g sugar
2 tsp sugar
1 bunch fresh coriander

Preparation

The day before ...

Heat the oil in a large casserole pan and add the onions. Stir until they soften.

Add the cumin, garlic, paprika and coriander and continue to cook for a few minutes.

Add the peppers until they soften, then add the veg stock, saffron, the chopped tomatoes and the bay and thyme bundle.

Leave to simmer for at least an hour on a low heat. Check the seasoning and add the vinegar and sugar - you don't want it to be sweet and sour, it's just to give it a little zing!

The next day ...

Warm the stew back up, add the chopped coriander leaves and set aside.

In an oven proof frying pan, add a good glug of olive oil and heat up. Add a couple of the eggs (you don't want to fill the pan with eggs, so you may have to do it in batches) and carefully add some of the stew to the pan around the eggs and place into a hot oven until the whites are cooked and the yolks are still runny.

Serve with crusty bread for dunkin'!

EGGS BENEDICT

{ It's only a once in a while treat, so try to put the bit about all that butter to the back of your mind. Make the sauce first. You can buy the sauce in some delis and some restaurants even use a bought in sauce. Lord knows how the shop bought stuff is made, the whole nature of this sauce stops it being able to withstand reheating. We make ours twice a day and use a flask to keep it warm, but not hot (otherwise the sauce will split), it'll be fine whilst you get the rest of the dish ready. }

Serves 4

200g sliced York ham
4 muffins – toasted and buttered
8 super fresh eggs
chopped chives – optional

The Hollandaise Sauce

1 x 250g block of unsalted butter – melted, hot to the touch
2 egg yolks
50ml water
few splashes of Tabasco
squeeze of lemon juice
salt and pepper
2 tsp white wine vinegar

Preparation

Toast and butter the muffins. Set the ham on top. Place the poached eggs on the ham, pour the sauce over and sprinkle with chives. How hard can it be? Now for the small matter of Hollandaise sauce and poaching eggs …

Preparation of the Hollandaise Sauce

Set a pan of simmering water going on the stove.
In a stainless steel mixing bowl, add the yolks, white wine vinegar and 50ml of boiling water.
Whisk over the pan of simmering water - don't let the bowl touch the water: that's too hot for the yolks.
The yolks should now be pale and foamy. Sit the bowl on a tea towel to keep steady and while whisking, drizzle the warm butter onto the yolk and if the sauce starts to look a little too thick, add a little more warm water.
Season with salt & pepper, stir in a splash of Tabasco to taste and a few drops of lemon juice.

I have a five point plan for poaching eggs! If any of the five points are not right, you'll have troublesome eggs …

Five Point Plan

1. Super fresh eggs; You can check how fresh the eggs are by cracking one on to a plate - the egg yolk should stand proud, the surrounding egg white should be thick and not spread out too much. Eggs that are getting on a bit have thin whites as the albumen has started to break down - these are the eggs that come out of the pan like a tatty old sock.

2. Crack the eggs into a small bowl or teacup first. This allows you to drop your egg into the water in one smooth movement. Also, not all eggs stay intact when you crack them open, so this way you'll know if you have a broken yolk. Another reason for dropping them into cups allows you to have your eggs at the ready for when the poaching water is at the perfect point.

3. Go Deep. I use a deep 2 litre pan, it's about 10 cm deep. I'd like to think that part of the reason for the lovely shape of a poached egg happens at this point. As it slowly falls down to the bottom of the pan, you can see it form the teardrop shape. Like a meteor entering the atmosphere with the fat round bit at the front and tailing off at the back.

4. Just-a-bit-more-than-simmering water. Not boiling, but not a flat surface either. I like to see a few bubbles just breaking the surface of the water. Too flat: the egg can just sit on the bottom and never gets up. Too furious: the tatty old sock is back.

5. Vinegar. The boring science bit. The acid helps to hold the protein together, blah blah blah - but it works. For a 2 litre pan, I add 200mls of vinegar. They usually take between 3 and 4 mins, but you can't set your watch by them. Your egg should float as it's almost ready, but to check, carefully lift the egg just out of the water with a slotted spoon and give it a gentle poke. If it feels a bit watery, pop it back in. You're looking for just set whites and super soft yolks.

WAFFLES

{ These are the waffles we make in the café on an industrial waffle iron, but I know for sure that they work on a domestic machine because most Sundays in our house, this is what we eat for breakfast at the crack of 11.30 am! The preparation is similar to making muffins, in that all dry ingredients go into one bowl and all wet ingredients go into another. }

Makes 6 waffles

The Dry Bowl
500g plain flour
5g salt
30g caster sugar
25g baking powder

The Wet Bowl
3 eggs
1 tsp vanilla extract
500g milk
100ml oil
125g butter

Preparation of the Dry Bowl

Run a whisk through the dry ingredients to help aerate the mix.

Preparation of the Wet Bowl

Melt the butter completely, but don't allow to get too hot.
Mix all the ingredients together.
Now, using a whisk, mix the two bowls together.
I find this mix easier to use if it's chilled first (make the night before!) as it's easier to spoon into the waffle maker.
If not, you'll just have to carefully pour the batter into the waffle iron.
If your maker has a setting, we bake our waffles at 220 C for 3 mins, remove carefully and sprinkle with a mix of icing sugar and ground cinnamon.

PORTUGUESE CUSTARD TARTS

{ You can skip the pastry bit in this recipe and just go for puff pastry instead.
I've made these before with puff, rough puff and even bought in pastry to make these, but they never seem quite right. We ate tons of these in Belem, Lisbon where the recipe is a closely guarded secret. I knew the pastry wasn't puff, yet it was flaky and definitely had layers. }

Makes 12

The Pastry
250g strong flour
125g cold water
5g salt
120g butter – soft, not melted

The Custard
900mls of milk
100mls double cream
3 strips of lemon peel
2 short cinnamon sticks
60g plain flour
20g cornflour
375g sugar
8 egg yolks
2 eggs

Preparation of the Pastry

Mix the salt into the flour, then work in the water and knead. It's a little like making pasta dough, only slightly softer.
Chill and rest for at least three hours.
Roll the dough out to the size of a 400mm x 300mm rectangle.
Spread with 60g of the soft butter – it needs to be easily spreadable, you don't want to tear any holes into your dough.
Then fold 1/3 of the dough in on itself (lengthways) and then fold the other 1/3 over (like a business letter).
Chill and rest.
Roll out again to the 400mm x 300mm rectangle.

Spread with the remaining 60g butter.

Carefully roll up the dough so that you end up with a 400mm long cylinder and then chill.

Cut the dough into 12 even pieces.

Spiral side down, press into a 12 hole deep muffin tray, so that the dough is evenly pressed into the mould.

Chill.

This is as close as I have got to cracking the recipe ...

Preparation

This is the easy bit, but it's important to let your flavours infuse in the milk and cream, so don't skimp on the simmering time.

Simmer the milk, cream, cinnamon and lemon peel together for 30 minutes on a really low heat.

In a separate bowl, mix the egg, yolks and flours together.

Pour the the liquid over the flour and egg and mix well, then pass through a sieve.

Pour into the lined muffin tins and bake at 210 C for 30 mins approx.

FRENCH TOAST

The Panini bread makes really good French toast, but any day old bread really will do.

Serves 4

3 eggs
200mls of cream
200mls of milk
1/2 tsp ground cinnamon
1 tsp vanilla extract
pinch of salt
melted butter
vegetable oil for frying

Preparation

Mix the eggs, cream, milk, cinnamon, vanilla and salt together.

Cut the bread and dip into the mix – leave for a couple of minutes or until you can feel that it is a bit heavier, soaking up the good stuff.

Heat the pan, add a splash of oil, then carefully place the soaked bread.

Wait until the you can see that the bread has formed a brown golden crust underneath, then flip over. Brush the top with a little melted butter, before flipping again and also brushing the other side with melted butter.

Dust with icing sugar and serve with maple syrup. In summer, we top with berries, in spring, with roasted rhubarb and in winter with chopped bananas.

SWEET BUN DOUGH

{ The mother recipe for a number of sweet treats, including Cinnamon Buns, Chelsea Buns, Donuts and Hot Cross Buns.
The dough may seem a little sticky and unmanageable, but once the bulk dough has been chilled, it'll be a lot easier to handle. }

500g flour
10g yeast
125g unsalted butter
70g sugar
1 tsp salt
3 eggs
200ml milk approx

Preparation

Add the yeast to the milk and add beaten eggs. Set aside.

Weigh the flour, salt, sugar and diced chilled butter into the bowl of a free standing mixer. Start the mixture off with the paddle attachment until the butter is combined.

Switch the paddle to the dough hook, and on a low speed, add the milk, egg and yeast. Keep mixing on a low speed for 5 to 7 mins until you have a smooth elastic dough. It should be sticky, but not too wet. If that's the case, add a little more flour and continue kneading.

Cover and allow to prove until doubled. Knock the dough back down, wrap and chill for an hour or two.

It'll continue rising again slowly in the fridge, so knock back down again and turn out onto a floured work top.

Roughly shape into a thick rectangle, ready to roll into your desired bun/donut ...

CINNAMON BUNS

Makes a dozen rolls from the Sweet Bun Dough recipe

	Glaze:
100g soft, not melted butter	125g melted butter
2 tbsp ground cinnamon	375g icing sugar
1 tbsp ground cardamom	100ml evaporated milk
175g soft brown sugar	1 tsp vanilla extract
	1 tsp ground cinnamon

Preparation

Roll the dough out to a large rectangle, 30cm x 60cm approx.

Spread the surface of the dough with the softened butter, then sprinkle the ground spices evenly across the dough. Sprinkle with the brown sugar and then start to roll the dough gently so that you end up with a 60cm long 'swiss roll' of dough...

Do your best to manipulate the cylinder into an even thickness, then measure out 12 even pieces of dough before cutting them into 12 even slices.

Into a tray (30cm x 42cm x 3cm deep approx.) lined with greaseproof paper, place the rolls cut side up. Try to evenly space them in the tin as they will grow and butt up to each other as they bake. Pre heat the oven to 180 C.

Cover and leave to prove until they have doubled. Into the oven for 25 mins, turning halfway to be sure they bake evenly.

Lift them out of the tray (still on the greaseproof paper) and leave to rest on a cooling rack. I prefer to leave them as a sheet of conjoined buns and tear each one away as you want it, so that they don't dry out.

For the glaze, simply melt the butter completely and combine all the ingredients together.

Whilst the buns are still warm and the glaze is still runny, drizzle with the glaze and allow the mix to seep in before serving.

LEMONY CHELSEA BUNS

Makes a dozen rolls from the Sweet Bun Dough recipe

150g lemon curd (homemade or shop bought is fine)
100g soft brown sugar
200g raisins or sultanas
75g mixed peel
2 tbsp mixed spice

Glaze:
100g apricot jam
100ml water

Preparation

As for the cinnamon buns, but start with the lemon curd in place of the butter and spread it evenly across the rolled out dough.

Then scatter the remaining ingredients evenly, roll up, divide and place in the tray leaving to prove and bake as before.

To glaze, heat the jam and water together, pass through a sieve to remove lumps and brush the glaze all over the warm buns.

GRANOLA

{ In the café we serve the granola with honey, a pot of yogurt and whatever fruit is in season - autumn and winter time we usually go for bananas or poached pears, summer time, there are usually plenty of berries about and in spring, we go for Yorkshire rhubarb. For years, I used to poach rhubarb, but there's a fine line between firm poached rhubarb and a pan of mush. More recently, I discovered roasting the rhubarb in a little sugar left you with firmer rhubarb and delicious sticky roasting juices. }

Mix and match with the dried fruit if you like and make sure you use the nice big jumbo oats. There's a lot of shaking n' tossing making granola and the little oats tend to turn into toasted crumbs at the bottom of your cereal bowl.

Serves 10

250g maple syrup	25g flaked almonds
50g caster sugar	25g whole almonds
50ml sunflower oil	40g coconut - dessicated
1 tsp vanilla extract	25g coconut chips
250g jumbo oats	1 tsp ground cinnamon
80g mixed seeds	75g dried cranberries
75g pecans	75g raisins/ sultanas

Preparation

Set the oven to 160 C.
Combine all ingredients in a large mixing bowl.
Toss together well, then spread out into a clean roasting tray. Try not to have the mix too deep in the tray, a thin layer is better for toasting.
Every 5 to 10 minutes, remove from the oven and break up with a spoon. Repeat this until the mix is a nice golden brown.
Allow to cool before adding your dried fruit.
Keeps really well in an air tight container for a couple of weeks.

Roasted Rhubarb

There are no exact measurements for this. It depends how thick your rhubarb is for a start.
As a general guide …
Wash your rhubarb well, cut into 3 inch chunks and rinse quickly again and drain. While the rhubarb is still wet, toss in enough sugar to lightly coat the rhubarb. Spread out onto a roasting tray (again, a single layer is best) and roast at 200 C.
After 10 mins, turn the tray around and keep an eye on it after that. It's ready when the rhubarb has just a bit of give in it, remove from the oven and allow to cool in the tray. The residual heat will carry on cooking it a little more after coming out of the oven.
You can add finely chopped fresh ginger into the mix as well if you like.

RASPBERRY & LEMON MUFFINS

{
A simple quick-to-knock-up recipe. We use homemade lemon curd (recipe on page 181), but you can use a jar of shop bought lemon curd. The crumble mix isn't necessary, but it adds a lovely contrast in texture - the crunchy oaty topping versus the moist chewy inside of the muffin.
}

Makes 6 big 'uns!

Dry bowl
270g plain flour
2 1/2 tsp baking powder
1/4 tsp salt

Wet bowl
2 eggs
170g sugar
70g butter
190ml milk
zest of lemon
2 tbsp lemon curd
100g fresh raspberries

Crumble mix
150g flour
75g diced cold butter
50g jumbo oats
50g soft brown sugar
1/2 tsp ground cinnamon

Preparation

Make the crumble mix by rubbing together the butter and flour, then add the spice, sugar and oats.
Sieve the baking powder, flour and salt together and set aside.
In the wet bowl, melt the butter and add to the remaining wet ingredients.
Loosely fold the dry ingredients into the wet bowl.
Spoon the mix into a tray lined with muffin papers and heap some of the crumble mix on top.
Bake at 170 C for 20 - 25 mins.

WHOLEGRAIN PANCAKES

{ Don't be put off by the 'wholegrain' bit (equally, you may even be turned on by the 'wholegrain' bit - wholegrains might be your thing). All I'm saying is, that looking at the ingredients list, you don't expect to be getting such a moist puffy pancake, but you do! I've tried loads of pancake recipes and even the kids agree that these are the best (wholegrains are definitely NOT their thing). }

Serves 6

The Dry Bowl
240g *white soft flour*
100g *buckwheat flour*
60g *spelt flour*
75g *oats*
3 *tbsp sugar*
2 *tbsp baking powder*
1/2 *tsp salt*

The Wet Bowl
3 *eggs*
360ml *milk*
360ml *buttermilk*
3 *tbspn butter*

To Serve
maple syrup
toasted flaked almonds
sliced bananas
icing sugar

Preparation

A simple all-wet-ingredients-added-to-all-dry-ingredients type recipe. Just be sure to run a whisk through the dry ingredients to make sure everything is evenly incorporated and then the same with the wet ingredients before the two bowls are added together.

I have a heavy flat griddle that sits on top of the gas hob for these. Get it nice and hot, lightly oil and turn down to a medium heat before adding the pancakes.

When you see the sides of the pancake look cooked, flip over and finish the other side off. I like to add a little butter to the skillet at this stage.

Pop a thin knife into the pancake to see if it is cooked to the centre. Then remove from the pan, dust with icing sugar, drizzle with maple syrup and top with bananas and toasted flaked almonds.

HERBY MUSHROOMS ON TOAST

{ You need nice big flat mushrooms for this recipe and ideally, with some cup on the edges of the mushrooms to hold in the herb butter. Some of the butter will inevitably come off the mushrooms when cooking, so make sure you have a tray with sides to catch the juices - you can pour the juices from the tray over the mushrooms before you serve. }

Serves four for brunch on top of buttered granary toast …

16 flat mushrooms
salt & pepper
a litttle truffle oil
thick sliced granary bread

Herb Butter
30g fresh tarragon
50g flat leaf parsley
25g chives
20g fresh basil leaves
1 clove garlic
300g of salted butter (you can use soya spread to keep it vegan)

Preparation

Melt the butter carefully until just melted, not red hot.

Wash and roughly chop all the herbs and the garlic.

Place all the herbs into a blender and gradually add all the melted butter.

Place the mushrooms upside down on a tray, trim the stalks if large and season with salt & pepper.

Spoon the herb butter over the mushrooms and bake in the oven at 200c for 20 to 25 mins (depending on the thickness).

When ready, toast and butter the bread, sit the mushrooms on top, and drizzle the juices over - the toast soaks the juices up nicely. If you have it, drizzle with just a few drops of truffle oil. Not just a few drops because it's so expensive, but a few drops is all you need. There's a fine line between bringing out the flavour of the mushrooms and making your mushrooms taste of gasoline!

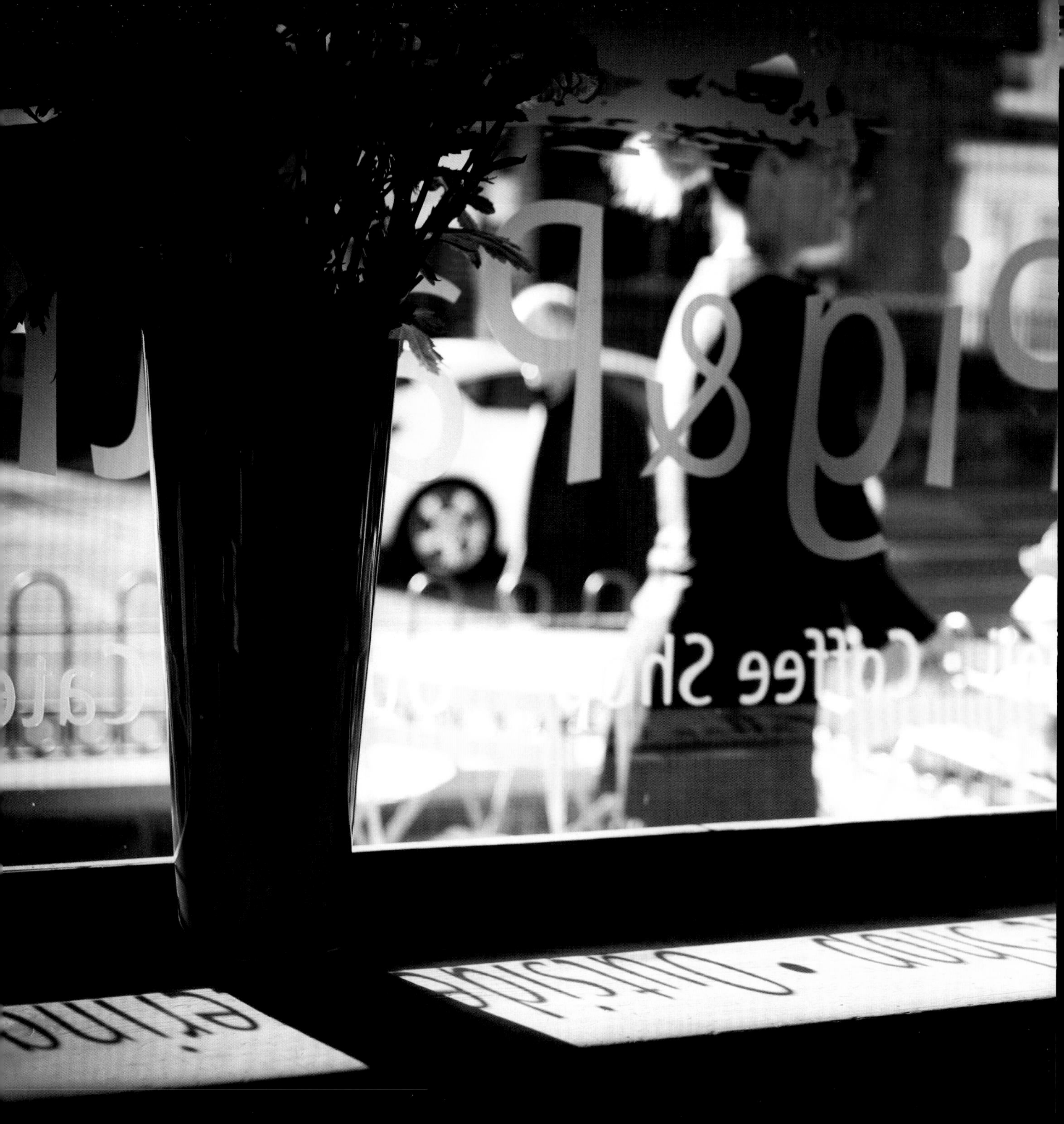

THREE SALADS

Really fresh ingredients and well made dressings are key to great salads. The following salads are all really designed to be presented in a big bowl and shared out at a BBQ, party, etc to accompany the main dish. However, sometimes it's nice to just sit down with a little selection of tasty salads and some good bread.

FRUITY COUSCOUS

Serves 16 to 20

350g couscous
50g pistachio nuts
400g tin chickpeas – drained and rinsed
50g soaked raisins
50g dried apricots
1 bunch spring onions
4 celery stalks
50g bunch parsley
25g bunch mint
25g bunch coriander
1 garlic clove – crushed
150ml extra virgin olive oil
1/2 lemon - juiced
sea salt & pepper

Preparation

Cook the couscous and cool.

Soak the raisins and apricots.

Meanwhile, chop all the herbs and thinly slice the spring onions and washed celery.

Make the dressing by crushing the garlic, squeezing the lemons and mixing together with the olive oil, salt & pepper.

Drain the fruit, chop the apricots and toss all the ingredients together.

CAROLINA STYLE COLESLAW

A world apart from your 'regular' coleslaw. Sweet 'n' tangy and with the addition of peppers. This slaw is perfect with pulled pork either in the bun with the pork, or on the side ...

Serves 16 to 20

1 white cabbage – shredded
8 carrots – grated
1 thinly sliced onion
2 thinly sliced red peppers

Dressing

*1 **cup** sugar*
*1 **tsp** salt*
*1 **cup** veg oil*
*1 **tsp** English mustard*
*1 **tsp** celery salt*
*1 **cup** cider vinegar*

Preparation

Mix together the dressing ingredients, then add to the vegetables.

WATERMELON & GINGER SALAD

{ As soon as these are in season, we have this salad on just about every day (much to Sue's annoyance, "oh, melon again!") }

Serves 16 to 20

1 medium sized watermelon
50g fresh root ginger
1/2 bunch of fresh mint
100ml rice wine vinegar
150g caster sugar

Preparation

In a non reactive pan, simmer the vinegar and sugar together until the sugar has dissolved. Set aside and leave to cool.

Peel and finely chop the ginger and add to a large bowl.

Wash and pick the mint leaves and finely shred and add to the bowl.

Cut the melon in half and carefully cut away the skin. Cut the melon into large chunks and add to the mint and ginger.

Drizzle the sugar dressing over the melon, mint and ginger and toss together.

Serve immediately - this salad doesn't keep well. Within a few hours, the salad will be a watery mess.

TRUFFLE EGG TOAST

{ Take your cheese on toast to the next level … }

Serves 1

1 doorstop of white bread
2 egg yolks
mature Cheddar or Fontina cheese
sea salt & pepper
truffle oil

Preparation

Cut yourself a nice thick piece of white bread.
Using the end of a rolling pin, make a couple of dimples in the bread to sit the yolks in.
Cover the yolks and bread with cheese.
Into the oven at 200 C for about 6 to 7 mins, or under a medium grill until the cheese is starting to bubble up and the yolks are still runny.
Season, drizzle with truffle oil and serve with a dollop of mustard.

OUR WEEKDAY FOCACCIA BREAD FOR PANINI AND SANDWICHES

900g strong white flour

15g salt

15g sugar

15g yeast

25g extra virgin olive oil – plus more for the tin and drizzling over

500g water

Preparation

Set the yeast to bloom in the tepid water, olive oil and sugar.

Mix the salt into the flour and add the water. Knead well for 10 minutes.

Cover and bulk prove for 20 mins, turn out, dimple, fold and bulk prove again.

Roll or stretch out to the size of a 30cm x 42cm tin. Brush the top with a little olive oil and loosely cover with cling wrap.

Once it has doubled in size, it's ready to go in the oven. 200 C for 12 minutes, spin around and then a further 12 minutes.

Turn out onto a cooling rack and leave to cool right down before cutting into it. Makes 10 big sandwiches

Some of our popular sandwiches made with this bread ...

THE BRIE. L. T

Preparation

Brie (of course!) rocket (the lettuce bit) and sun blush tomatoes - these are much softer than sun dried tomatoes and have a more intense flavour than sliced fresh tomatoes. Sometimes we make these if we have a glut of tomatoes (especially if they're slightly over-ripe) by cutting into wedges, tossing in olive oil, herbs, salt and garlic and leaving them in the oven overnight on the pilot light. Slow roasted tomatoes with an intense hit!

THE B.A.F.T.A

bacon (crispy)
avocado (in the form of guacamole)
feta cheese
tomato (sliced fresh tomatoes)
aioli

Preparation

The bread for this one we lightly press under the Panini grill, then on one slice spread aioli, on the other spread the guacamole and then fill with feta, sliced tomatoes and bacon.

THE BIG SQUEAK

Named after the sound made by one of the main ingredients - Halloumi. The squeaky cheese.
Again, we lightly toast the bread, then, spread one with aioli, the other slice with sweet chilli sauce. Fill with some rocket, some grilled roasted peppers (tinned) and some grilled halloumi.

THE RORY MOTION

Name after our local artist/comedian/painter/poet's favourite sandwich. This one we serve hot. The mushrooms and the onions are hot, placed into the sandwich with the chilli sauce and the cheddar and then pressed in the Panini grill.

herb roasted mushrooms
mature cheddar cheese —thinly sliced
sweet chilli sauce
caramelised onions

"By naming a sandwich
after me, you've put me up there with
Leonardo DiCaprio, Michael Caine
and Dolly Parton, and their
sandwiches weren't even grilled ..."

Rory Motion

SAUSAGE ROLLS

{ Easy to make and essentially only two ingredients which is why it's so important to make sure those two ingredients are the best you can find.
Ask your butcher for best quality sausage meat or if there's a particular type of sausage you're really fond of, then simply squeeze the meat from the skin. Same thing! }

Makes 4

300g best puff pastry
400g sausage meat
egg yolk for sealing and
glazing

Preparation

Roll the puff pastry out to an even size of 25cm x 40cm.
Roll the sausage meat to 40cm in length and place on the edge of the puff pastry.
Roll the sausage meat in the puff pastry, until you come to the last couple of inches. Brush the last couple of inches of pastry with egg yolk to seal the seam.
Seam side down, cut the roll into four portions and seam side down, sit onto a lined baking tray.
Brush the sausage rolls with egg yolk and bake at 180 C for 35 to 40 mins.

QUICHE (GIVE QUICHE A CHANCE...)

Tasty, homely, versatile and the one menu item that's popular all year round - great for a picnic, a buffet, a light lunch, heated up for supper or eaten on the go. The fillings for these are endless really, basically, you need a really good cheese and some cooked vegetables or meat that goes well with the cheese:

Quiche Lorraine – Gruyere, lightly caramelised onions & smoky bacon

Stilton & broccoli

Smoked salmon, cream cheese & chives

Feta, olives, sun dried tomatoes & marinated artichokes

Dolcelatte, pear & hazelnut (sounds a little weird, but it's delicious!)

Serves 8

The Savoury Pastry

500g plain flour

250g unsalted butter

125ml water

7g salt

Preparation

Rub the butter, flour & salt together until it resembles fine breadcrumbs. Mix in the water and bring together on a floured worktop. Don't over work at this stage. Wrap, chill and rest for at least an hour.

Roll out to an even thickness and line your flan ring, carefully pushing the pastry right down into the corners, but be careful not to tear the pastry. Leave a good couple of centimetres of pastry overhanging the flan ring edges - do not trim this off yet. Chill for another hour while you get your fillings ready.

Line the pastry case with baking parchment, then fill with baking beans. Bake at 180 C for 30 mins approx. or until lightly golden around the edges and when you lift up the paper, the pastry doesn't look raw. Carefully lift out the beans and parchment and place the quiche base back into the oven for 5 to 10 mins to help cook the base (be careful at this point - too long and the base can still puff up and crack - game over!)

Fill the quiche with your fillings and then carefully pour over the custard. Bake at 170'c for 30 - 40 mins or until ready. Give the tray a light shake, your custard should have a firm wobble when ready and in no way should it look liquid at this point. If it does, back into the oven until it's ready.

When ready, leave to cool for 30 mins. Now you can trim the crust! Ideally with a small serrated knife, pushing against the edge of the flan ring or dish.

Depending on the filling, now is a good time to finish the quiche with a little grated parmesan. Done!

The Custard
250mls milk

250mls double cream

4 eggs

2 yolks

salt & pepper

Preparation

Mix together with a whisk to break through the eggs and then pass through a sieve.

CHORIZO SCOTCH EGGS

Serves 6

300g sausage meat
300g chorizo parilla sausages
chopped parsley
8 eggs
200ml milk
200g plain flour
300g breadcrumbs

Preparation

First, cook the eggs. Plunge the eggs into boiling water and continue to boil for 7 minutes. Run under cold water for a few minutes. Peel and then pop back in the fridge for a bit.

Mix the sausage meat with the diced skinned chorizo and the chopped parsley. Chill.

Divide the sausage meat into 100g lumps approx and between two sheets of cling film, pat the meat into a flat layer large enough to wrap around the peeled egg. Sit the egg in the middle of the meat and pull the cling film and meat around the egg. Twist the clingfilm at the top to hold the meat encapsulated egg in place. Chill.

Take three bowls. One with seasoned flour, one with the remaining 2 eggs and the milk and the last with the bread crumbs. Carefully (and ideally with a partner/friend/helper/lover) unwrap the meaty eggs, dip in the flour and shake off the excess, into the eggy mix and finally into the breadcrumbs. Sometimes you may need to repeat the egg and breadcrumb bit. Chill.

Set the fryer at 180 C and carefully place into the oil for 6 to 8 minutes (depends how even you managed to get your sausage meat, the thick bits take longer).

We serve these with a dollop of aioli for dipping.

PULLED PORK

This is a big recipe: ideal for a big bbq or a party. You're going to need a big pan and a big tray and lots of room in the fridge for the overnight rub. Alternatively, get a small joint in, make the same amount of 'rub' and just save the remainder in an airtight container for the next time ...

The Rub
1/2 cup brown sugar
2 tsp white pepper
2 tsp garlic powder
2 tsp cayenne
2 tsp salt
1/2 tsp ground cumin

The Roast
1 pork shoulder - bone in
5 - 6kg approx
(ask your butcher to score the skin)
3 onions
8 carrots
1 head of celery

The Sauce
1 1/2 cups cider vinegar
1/2 cup Colmans mustard
1 cup ketchup
1/3 cup brown sugar
2 garlic cloves
1 tsp salt
1 tsp cayenne pepper
1/2 tsp ground black pepper

Preparation

Make the rub by mixing all ingredients together.

Rub all over the pork joint, cover and chill overnight (sit it on a tray to catch any liquid that comes out overnight).

Line the base of a roasting tray with thickly sliced onion, carrot & celery. Sit the pork on top, pour about half an inch of water in the base of the tray and cover with foil.

Roast for 9 hours approx. at 160 C. When ready, the bone should be easy to move within the meat. The meat should also be tender and easy to pull apart. Leave to cool and rest for an hour.

Get yourself two bowls, one for the meat that you're going to keep and one for the bones and gristle.

Pour all the juices into a pot and cool. Allow to go completely cold and pick off the fat. You should be left with a tasty pork jelly.

Make 'the sauce' by simmering all the ingredients together. Add the pork jelly to the sauce, then stir in the picked meat. Ready! At this stage I like to add hot sauce such as Franks or Tabasco.

RIBOLLITA

A hearty summer soup/delicious supper and an excellent way of using up the ends of good bread. The little pieces of bread soak up all the good stuff and help to thicken the soup. I don't think it's traditional to serve Parmesan with this soup, but I think that it goes great with beans and cabbage.

Serves 6 to 8

4 sticks of celery

4 carrots

2 leeks

2 medium onions

1 head of cavolo nero (usually only available in the summer months, if you can't get a hold of this, I use spring greens or the outer leaves of Savoy)

4 cloves of garlic

2 x 400g tins of chopped tomatoes

2 x 400g tins of cannellini beans (or little butterbeans)

2 litres of vegetable stock

400g stale/yesterdays bread

bay leaf

100mls olive oil

salt and pepper

freshly chopped parsley

freshly grated Parmesan

Preparation

Start by tearing your leftover bread into roughly 1 inch little cubes into a bowl. Drizzle with the olive oil and set aside.

In a large pan, sweat down the celery, onions, carrots, leeks and garlic until they start to soften.

Add the beans, tomatoes, bay leaf and enough stock to just cover the ingredients in the pan. You may not need all the stock yet, but as it simmers, you may need to add a little more.

Once the vegetables are cooked, you can either leave it nice and chunky as it is, or, I like to take a couple of ladles of the soup out of the pan, blend this up until smooth and then add back to the pan of chunky soup so it's a little bit chunky, a little bit smooth!

Finally, stir in the bread (you may not need all of this), the cabbage (which has been blanched and chopped), the parsley and, if required, a little more stock. Check the seasoning and serve up. Sprinkle with Parmesan if you like.

ITALIAN CHICKPEA SOUP

Most broths, I find, tend to have a wintery feel about them, with maybe the exception of Ribollita. This broth is popular and great to eat in summer and winter – maybe because of its Mediterranean origin, it plants the seed in my mind that therefore it must be summery. It doesn't look classically Mediterranean, unless I'm making it wrong, but either way it tastes great and is dead simple to make.
Really good tinned chickpeas are needed. Some, even tinned ones tend to be a little toothsome and no end of cooking gets them to soften. The ones we use are Spanish – they look bigger than most chickpeas you find, almost swollen in the brine they are preserved in it seems.

An approximate recipe for four portions

2 carrots

1 onion

3 sticks of celery

1 leek

2 cloves of garlic

400g tin of chickpeas

1 bay leaf

couple of sprigs of rosemary

2 plum tomatoes

enough vegetable stock to cover, plus a little more

olive oil

salt and pepper to taste (watch out, vegetable stocks, well most instant stocks can already be very salty)

Preparation

Chop the carrots, leek, celery and onion fairly chunky. Sweat down in some olive oil on a medium heat until they start to soften.
Add the garlic & chopped rosemary and cook out the garlic for a little while.
Add the chopped tomatoes and stir in the chickpeas. Cover with stock and throw in a bay leaf.
Leave to simmer gently for about an hour or until the vegetables are really tender.

CHICKEN SOUP AND DUMPLINGS

There's something very satisfying about making use of every part of something and this is one of those dishes. It's also a soup that tastes better the next day. When I was young, I remember my mum, my aunt and my gran all made this soup. When one of them made it, I'd cycle round and pick up some Tupperware tubs of it to deliver to the other two houses. (We all lived within 3 streets of each other). I'm not sure if it was just good old generosity or maybe a little bit of competitiveness that they used to always want to share their wares, but you were never allowed to say whose was the best (It was my Grans! Sorry mum).

A great soup to make the day after a roast chicken: pick every last morsel from the bird and make a stock from the carcass.
The dumplings look a bit weird, but they soak up all that chickenie goodness and they taste great. A real winter time soup.

Serves 6 to 8

2 sticks of celery
1 onion
2 cloves of garlic - crushed
2 carrots
1/2 a swede
1 large leek
50g red lentils (or you can use rice)

1 bay leaf
few sprigs of thyme
cooked chicken meat
homemade chicken stock
(enough to cover the ingredients, plus
an inch or two in the pan more)

Preparation

In a large pan, sweat down the vegetables in a little butter until they begin to soften.
Stir in the garlic, lentils, bayleaf and thyme, then add the stock.
Leave to simmer until the lentils and vegetables are fully cooked, then check the seasoning (if your stock was a little weak, add some of the instant type to make it a bit more gutsy).

The dumplings

2 large eggs

1/2 tsp salt

65g plain flour

Preparation

These come straight from the Claudia Roden Book of Jewish Food and like she says, don't expect neat round dumplings.

Beat into a smooth batter and drop into simmering chicken stock. When they rise, remove from the stock. When you're ready to eat the soup, add the dumplings and heat up along with the soup. Finish with freshly chopped parsley.

CURED PEA & HAM SOUP

{ We're very lucky to have such a great butcher on the street, especially as he gives us the knuckle ends of cured hams. When we get these, we freeze them until we have enough and then make the following soup. It's a Spanish recipe I think, thinner than the traditional pea and ham soup and maybe a little saltier too (this comes from the salty cured hams).
Cured ham ends are not easy to get your hands on. I remember Brindisa in Borough Market used to sell tubs of the trimmings cheaply, but if you can't get any, you can make your stock with a ham hock and when it comes to making the soup, add some pancetta to the vegetables as you sweat them down. }

No exact ingredients for this recipe, but like me, you'll just need to see how much ham stock you can make first …

First, make a stock with the ham ends by removing any surplus fat and simmering them with a little onion, garlic, thyme, bay leaf, carrot and celery. Pass and leave to chill, you can then pick off any fat that has risen to the top once it has gone cold.

Preparation

In a large pan sweat down some onion, carrot, and celery. When they begin to soften, add a little crushed garlic and some smoked paprika.

Stir in the peas and enough ham stock to cover plus an inch or two, add the bay leaf and thyme and leave to simmer until the vegetables have completely softened.

Remove the thyme and the bay and discard. Take out half of the soup and blend in a liquidiser until smooth and then add back to the rest of the soup.

The soup is now ready and at this stage, I like to add some crispy cured ham slices and if you have it, a couple of drops of truffle oil.

LENTIL & SPINACH SOUP WITH MOROCCAN SPICES & YOGURT

There's something very comforting and autumnal about lentils, but I also love this as a summery soup. For a lentil soup, it's not too heavy and is made lighter with the addition of spinach and a dollop of natural Greek yogurt.

Serves 4 to 6

1 tsp ground cumin

1 tsp smoked paprika (mild)

1 tsp Ras al Hanut

5 cloves of garlic

2 large white onions

1 green chilli

1 1/2 litres vegetable stock

1 x 200g bag of brown lentils

fresh coriander

bay leaf

olive oil

250g bag of baby spinach – washed and spun dry

salt and pepper

natural Greek yogurt

Preparation

Thinly slice the onion and sauté in the olive oil without colouring.

Add the chopped garlic, chopped chilli and the spices and mix in well.

Add the lentils, bay leaf and the vegetable stock and bring almost to the boil.

Simmer until the onions and lentils are tender, take off the heat and remove the bay.

Remove about a third of the soup and blend until smooth, then add back to the rest of the soup. You may need to add more stock/water for a lighter consistency, but I really like it when these kind of soups look half-smooth-half-chunky-broth-like.

To serve, add the washed baby spinach to the soup (it looks like loads at first, but it wilts right down), serve in bowls with a dollop of yogurt, a drizzle of olive oil and some chopped coriander.

PROVENÇAL TOMATOES

We serve these with gnocchi, but they're great on their own, served on top of toast as a lunch or light supper dish. The smell of these cooking will knock you out!

Serves four

8 large plum tomatoes – ripe, or slightly over-ripe are best

1/2 bunch basil

2 tsp herbes de Provence

extra virgin olive oil

4 cloves garlic

cracked black pepper

sea salt

200mls double cream

100g finely grated Parmesan cheese

Preparation

Cut the tomatoes in half, lengthways and place into a large bowl.

Season with the salt and pepper, toss with a good glug of olive oil.

Chop the garlic finely and roughly chop the basil. Add into the bowl and add the herbes de Provence and mix well.

Place the tomatoes into a baking tray (the tray/dish should be just big enough to sit the tomatoes in nice and close together without too much blank space), 'cut side up' and then, scrape out all the herbs and bits from the bowl and add to the top of the tomatoes.

Into a hot oven, about 200 C for about 30 mins. The herbs on the tomatoes should just be starting to singe and a good amount of juice should have come out of the tomatoes. Remove from the oven.

Add the cream over the tomatoes and sprinkle with finely grated Parmesan.

Back into the oven until the cream is starting to bubble and blister, about 10 to 12 mins should do it. Then serve over thick cut, hot, buttered toast.

SALT COD FRITTERS

{ We don't use the traditional air dried salt cod for this recipe. 1, it takes forever to soak and 2, it's really hard to get hold of. I like this recipe, as nothing is wasted. The poaching liquor from the fish is used to cook the potatoes so none of the tasty fish flavours are lost.

We use fresh cod, haddock or whiting fillet. Generously sprinkle with table salt, wrap and chill for a couple of days. Then, soak in cold water overnight, rinse and pat dry. }

Serves 4

250g white fish
250g potato cut into large dice
1 bay leaf
few sprigs of thyme

500mls milk
2 cloves peeled garlic
50g fresh flat leaf parsley
1/2 an onion

Preparation

So, once you've rinsed and dried your fish, place into a bowl and set aside.

Place the herbs and garlic into a pan with the milk and simmer for 10 - 15 mins.

While still hot, pour the milk over the fish and quickly cover the bowl with cling film tightly. The fish will cook in the residual heat.

Strain the milk from the fish and pour over the raw potatoes in a pan. Set the fish aside, pick out the herbs and garlic and add to the potatoes.

Simmer the potatoes until tender, pick out the herbs and mash the potatoes while they are still hot.

Wash, dry and chop the parsley and grate the onion (squeeze out the juice).

Mix the fish, parsley, grated onion and mashed potato together.

Put spoonfuls of the mix into a 2 inch ring and push down.

Toss the fritters lightly in flour and pan fry in a hot non stick pan.

Serve with aioli and lemon.

SPINACH PANCAKES WITH HALLOUMI & LIME BUTTER

{ Taken and adapted from the Ottolenghi book, Plenty. }

Serves 4

500g large leaf spinach
25g butter (to cook the spinach)
salt & pepper
110g plain flour
1 1/2 tbsp baking powder
1/2 tsp salt
1 bunch spring onions (about 8 large spring onions)

2 green chillies finely chopped
1 tsp toasted ground cumin
2 eggs
50g melted butter
2 egg whites – whipped, soft peaks
1 x 200g block of Halloumi

Lime & Coriander Butter

125g butter – soft
2 limes zested & juiced
1/2 bunch coriander
2 cloves of garlic
salt & pepper
1/2 tsp dried chilli flakes (or one small fresh green chilli)

Preparation

Pick through the spinach, discard the stems and wash in plenty of cold water. Heat up a large pan on the stove, add a knob of butter and quickly toss in the spinach.

Season in the pan and remove as soon as it has wilted. Place into a colander until cool enough to handle. Repeat this stage in batches if you need to. Squeeze the spinach when cool to remove any excess liquid and then roughly chop. Set aside.

You'll need three bowls. One for all the dry (flour, baking powder, cumin, etc), one for the wet (melted butter, eggs and the cooked chopped spinach) and one for whipping the whites.

Combine the dry bowl with the wet bowl and fold in the egg whites carefully.

Prepare the butter by combining all the ingredients into the bowl of a food processor with the blade attachment fitted. Alternatively, you can chop the garlic, chilli and coriander really finely and beat into the butter by hand. Slowly add the lime juice once everything has been added. Chill until needed.

Heat up a large, flat, heavy bottomed non-stick pan. Add a little oil to the pan and then drop large dessert spoonfuls of mix into the pan. Space well apart, as they will spread out a little. When you see the edges of the pancake begin to cook, flip the pancake over and turn down the heat. Check the pancakes are ready by inserting a small knife into the centre - they should be moist, but no signs of wet pancake mix.

Place the cooked pancakes on a plate and keep warm for a couple of minutes.

Cut the halloumi into 8 slices, and place into the hot pan - you may need a splash of oil, depending on how non stick your pan is. Caramelise each side and sit on top of the pancakes.

In the same pan, add the lime butter until melted and frothy (don't let your pan get too hot - the butter will burn!), and drizzle over the pancakes and Halloumi and serve.

ANDY'S FISHCAKES

750g *salmon fillet*
500g *Desirée potatoes*
3 *bunches spring onions*
1 tsp *English mustard*
2 *lemons*
1 *bay leaf*
1 tbsp *chopped dill*
2 tbsp *chopped parsley*

Coating

4 tbsp *flour*
100ml *milk*
4 *eggs*
200g *breadcrumbs*

Preparation

Line a deep dish with a large sheet of foil. Place the salmon fillet on the foil and season with salt and pepper. Add a splash of white wine, half the lemon juice and wrap the fillets up in the foil. Bake at 200 C for 10 - 15 mins depending upon how thick your salmon is. Leave to cool in the foil.

Peel and boil the potatoes in salted water, strain well and break up with a fork. Leave to cool.

Flake up the salmon into a mixing bowl with the potatoes, herbs, chopped spring onions, mustard and the rest of the lemon juice. Check the seasoning and then shape into 6 - 8 fishcakes. Pushing the fishcake mix into a ring helps to get a firmer shape.

In three separate bowls, have the flour in one, the beaten eggs and milk in one and the breadcrumbs in another. Preheat the oven to 200 C.

Take the shaped fishcake and place into the flour and shake off any excess, then into the egg mix and then finally into the breadcrumbs making sure all is covered. Repeat with each fishcake (if you can get a volunteer at this stage, it'll stop your fingers turning into corn dogs).

In a heavy pan, on a medium heat, add a good amount of vegetable oil (about 3mm deep). Carefully place the half of the fishcakes into the pan and cook until golden and flip over and repeat. Place on a tray whilst you repeat with the other fishcakes. Place the tray into the oven for 10 - 12 mins.

Serve with a chunky tartare sauce, lemon and a crisp salad.

AVOCADO TOAST

{ Do we really need a recipe for this?

Every hipster café in London has its version of Avocado Toast. What's all the fuss about I thought? Well, get it right and it's damn delicious.

The key is really good bread and really good avocados. The good bread may be easier to find than the good avocados, now that we are lucky enough to have so many good bakeries in recent years. Avocados, more troublesome than getting a ripe banana when you want one. }

I've heard top tips of leaving avo's under tea towels on a shelf or placing them in your airing cupboard, but who wants to be messing and waiting around for an avocado to make its mind up? Buy the avocados when they are ready to eat (they should 'give a little' when you give them a gentle squeeze) and then just eat them the same day.

Serves one hungry hipster...

2 fairly thick slices of sourdough

1 ripe avocado

1 lemon

chilli oil

fresh coriander

sea salt and cracked black pepper

Preparation

Prepare the avocado by cutting into quarters, remove the stone and carefully peel back the skin.

Toast the sourdough slices - do not butter!

Place the avocados on the toast and lightly smash in with a fork.

Season the avocados with salt and pepper, drizzle lightly with a squeeze of lemon juice, drizzle with a little chilli oil and sprinkle with picked coriander leaves.

Serve immediately (and be careful not to get crumbs in your freshly waxed moustache).

There, I was right. You don't really need a recipe for avocado toast ...

ANDY'S ROSEMARY & CHILLI POLENTA CHIPS

{ We serve these with the mushroom ragout on the next page ... }

Serves 4

1 litre of light vegetable stock
250g polenta
50g grated fresh Parmesan
25g butter
3 tsp chopped rosemary
1 – 2 red chillis – deseeded and
finely chopped

Preparation

Place the stock in a pan and bring to the boil with the crushed garlic.

Slowly pour in the polenta and keep stirring. Once it starts to bubble and thicken, turn down to the lowest heat.

Add in the rosemary and chilli and stir well. Once the polenta is thick, smooth and not grainy, take off the heat and add the Parmesan and butter.

Line a baking tray with cling film and spread the polenta evenly and leave it to set.

Take the polenta out of the tray and cut into thick chips. Heat a heavy non stick frying pan, add a little oil and fry the polenta until crispy and golden on all sides.

FIELD MUSHROOM & ARTICHOKE RAGOUT

Serves 4

10g dried cepes
500g field mushrooms
olive oil
2 large shallots
3 cloves garlic
1/4 bunch of thyme
4 artichoke hearts – tinned are fine
200ml red wine
400g chopped tinned tomatoes
1/2 tblsp chopped tarragon
1/4 bunch flat leaf parsley
little splash of truffle oil, optional

Preparation

Rinse and soak cepes in just enough water to cover (overnight ideally, which will result in a nice meaty stock).
Thinly slice and sweat the shallots in a little olive oil, until softened, then add the garlic.
Thickly slice the field mushrooms and add to the shallots and cook under a lid until the mushrooms have softened.
Add the thyme and the red wine. Turn up the heat to reduce the wine down to virtually nothing, then add the cepes and the soaking liquor, the tarragon, sliced artichokes and the tomatoes and leave to simmer on a low heat for 30 - 45 mins.
As it's cooking, you may need to top up with a little water or a light vegetable stock. Check for seasoning and finish with chopped parsley and a splash of truffle oil.

LEMONADE

Don't expect this to be carbonated, nor super sweet for that matter. But chilled and made right, this is unbelievably refreshing. People ask for the recipe and when I tell them, they generally look disappointed, 'is that it?!'

Yes, that's it! You're in luck, kids love it, it's cheap and the kids love making it! It makes them feel like little alchemists. Serve with ice and fresh mint and once you've nailed it, there are some minor variations at the end of the recipe ...

Makes 5 to 6 glasses

150g caster sugar
1 litre water
175mls lemon juice
ice and mint to serve
that's it!

Preparation

First off, zest the lemons. Lightly though, you don't want the bitter pith getting into the drink. Measure out the water and the sugar and place into a non reactive pan with the zest. Bring almost to the boil and simmer for 20 mins. Leave to cool.

Meanwhile, juice the lemons and set aside. Once the sugar, water and zest has cooled down, add the lemon juice. Don't worry if any pips get in, we'll sieve those out later on. Cover and chill overnight.

Pass through a sieve and decant into bottles.

Yes, that's it!

Ginger & Lemon Grass

Substitute some of the lemons for two limes, juiced and zested, then make up the rest of the 175ml of juice required with lemons.

Into the base mix of sugar, zest and water, add 6 stalks of bashed lemon grass, 50g of fresh grated ginger and if you can get them, a couple of lime leaves.

Pink lemonade

Same as the first recipe, but on day two, blend the lemonade with 200g of fresh strawberries and pass through a sieve.

Blueberry and Vanilla

As for the pink lemonade, but substituting the strawberries for fresh or frozen blueberries instead. In place of the caster sugar, use vanilla sugar if you have it, or add a scraped vanilla bean to the mix.

SHAKES!

We have the old fashioned spindle type machine, which means all flavourings need to be preblended. You can use a liquidiser or blender at home which means you won't need to be so particular on how small your ingredients are, depending upon how powerful your blender is.

Here's our recipe sheet, each for one serving in a frosted glass with an extra wide straw.

Play around with the milk depending upon how thick you like your shakes. Always use full fat milk - it's pointless lying to yourself with semi skimmed when you're chucking in big scoops of ice cream!

(We have Iain & Kath who have The Pig & Pastry in Petersham (Sydney, Australia) to thank for the Gingerbread and the Strawberry milkshake recipes. Thanks bruv, they're awesome!)

Malted Chocolate

1 scoop vanilla ice cream

1 scoop chocolate ice cream

2 tbsp Malteser crumbs

1 tbsp Ovaltine (or Horlicks)

top up with milk

Oreo

2 scoops vanilla ice cream

2 tbsp Oreo crumbs

top up with milk

Strawberry & Vanilla

2 scoops strawberry ice cream

big glug o' strawberry purée

(some purée into the glass as well)

shot of vanilla syrup

top up with milk

Gingerbread

2 scoops ice cream

*1 tsp spice mix ***

1 tbsp gingernut biscuit crumbs

1 tsp ground ginger

top up with milk

(sprinkle gingernuts on top as well)

*Spice mix is made of equal quantities of ground ginger, ground cinnamon and caster sugar.

RORY MOTION

£175
Reduced to feed
artists guiness
cake addiction

P B & J SHORTBREAD

{ The 'J' stands for Jam, not Jelly. Jelly, that would be ridiculous. }

Makes 15

Shortbread Base
125g caster sugar
425g flour
1/2 tsp salt
115g butter
1 egg

Preparation

Rub together the butter, sugar, salt and flour until fine.
Work in the egg until it comes together.
Press into a 33cm x 23 cm baking pan (lined with greaseproof - this'll make lifting out easier) and then chill while you get the rest ready.

Peanut Butter Bit
230g butter
365g peanut butter
300g icing sugar
1/2 tsp vanilla extract

In a free standing mixer add the soft (not melted) butter, peanut butter, icing sugar and vanilla extract with the paddle beater attachment.
Cover the bowl with a tea towel to prevent yourself getting consumed in a cloud of icing sugar. Start the machine off slow to begin with, then turn it up and beat until smooth and fluffy. It should look a bit like cupcake frosting.
While still soft, spread over the shortbread base and chill.

The Jam Bit

Enough good quality jam to spread a thin layer over the pb bit and the crumble bit (too much and it will ooze out and burn around the edges).

Crumb Top
125g flour
1/4 tsp salt
1/2 tsp baking powder
1/4 tsp bi carb
1/4 tsp cinnamon
70g Demerara sugar
65g oats
85g butter

Preparation

Put all ingredients in a bowl and rub together. The mixture doesn't have to be so fine, it's kinda nice to have clumpy bits on top.
Into a pre heated oven at 175 C for 25 to 30 mins.
Leave to cool completely, ideally for a few hours, before turning out and cutting into squares.
Makes 16 single servings or 40 party sized bites.

S'MORES

{
These aren't really true S'mores. S'mores are usually a campfire treat of toasted marshmallows and a piece of chocolate between a couple of Graham crackers. I've never seen Graham crackers over here –
the nearest thing is probably a digestive – but this recipe is better than any bought in version and is well worth having a go at.
It'll feel like there's nowhere near enough liquid to bring all the ingredients together, but there is! The key I think, is to have the butter as soft as you can get it without melting it.
}

Makes 12

Graham Crackers

195g plain flour, plus more for working
195g granary flour
1/2 tsp salt
1 tsp baking soda
1 tsp ground cinnamon
230g unsalted butter, softened
165g soft light-brown sugar
2 tbs high-quality honey

Marshmallows

450g sugar – hard ball (127 C)
9 leaves of soaked gelatin
(soaked in 140ml cold water)
1 tsp of vanilla essence
3 egg whites – whisk to stiff peaks
1 tsp glucose powder
50/50 mix of icing sugar & cornflour to
stop the marshmallows sticking

Preparation of the Graham Crackers

Rub everything together – like making shortbread.
Bring together and roll out between two sheets of parchment.
Keeping the rolled out dough on the parchment, slide onto a flat baking tray.
Bake for approx. 15 mins or until browning around the edges.
Take out of the oven and slide onto a flat worktop.
Cut, trim and portion the biscuits whilst still warm.
Leave the biscuits to cool and go crisp(ish).

Preparation of the Marshmallows

Soak the gelatin in 150ml cold water.

Line a 25cm x 30cm baking tray with cling film and brush with vegetable oil, then dust liberally with the cornflour and icing sugar mix.

In a super clean, dry and grease free pan, add the sugar, glucose and 300mls water.

In a free standing mixer (also super clean), get the egg whites whisking, full steam ahead until they reach stiff peaks.

Pop the thermometer in the sugar pan until it reaches 127 C ('hard ball' stage).

Add gelatin leaves (they should be soft and squidgy by now) and the water that they were soaking in, into the syrup. CAREFUL! The pan will spit at this stage as you carefully stir the gelatin into the syrup (it will also smell weird - try not to think about it!).

Start the whisk again whilst you drizzle in the syrup and continue to whisk until the mix is smooth, glossy and thick (about 5 - 7 minutes).

Pour into the prepared tray and smooth over with a spatula.

Leave to chill before cutting up into squares.

Toss the squares in some more of the icing sugar and cornflour mix to prevent them from sticking.

Milk Chocolate Ganache
200g best quality milk chocolate
100g double cream

Preparation

In a bowl over a pan of simmering water (not touching the water), stir the chocolate & cream together until completely melted, smooth and glossy. Leave to cool slightly.

Assemble Your S'mores …

Ideally, you'll have portioned your marshmallow and crackers into fairly equal sizes.

Next, carefully and lightly toast your marshmallow with the blowtorch.

Place a dollop of ganache on the marshmallow and finally sandwich between the two crackers.

LITTLE CHEESECAKES

{ Fairly labour intensive are these little tarts - so much so, that we only make them on Saturdays. There's sweet pastry to make, blind baking the tarts, cheesecake mix to make and bake and then there's the toppings ... but they're oh so worth it! }

Makes 12

The Sweet Pastry
250g flour
60g sugar
160g unsalted butter
2 yolks
25ml water approx.
pinch of salt

The Cheesecake Mix
250g cream cheese
70g sugar
10g cornflour
1 egg
1/2 tsp vanilla extract
1/4 vanilla pod
100ml whipping cream

Preparation of pastry cases

Rub the butter, sugar, salt & flour together.
Fold in the yolks and the water to bring together - don't overwork at this stage - form into a ball, wrap and chill for at least an hour.
Roll out the pastry to the thickness of a pound coin, cut out circles big enough to fit into a muffin tin, gently push the pastry into the tin and chill.
Sit little foil bean bags into the pastry cases and bake at 170 C for 25 - 30 mins.

Preparation of cheesecakes

Beat the cream cheese, egg, lemon zest, sugar and cornflour together with the vanilla extract.
Lightly whip the cream and fold into the cheesecake mix.
Spoon into the pre-baked pastry cases and bake at 170'c for 25 to 30 mins.
Leave to chill.
At this point, they're ready to eat as they are. If you want to take them to another level, here are some tasty toppings ...

LIMONCELLO MERINGUE PIE

The Lemon Curd Bit

30g butter

3 lemons zest & juice

125g sugar

4 eggs

Preparation

Put all the ingredients into a stainless steel bowl. Sit the bowl over a pan of simmering water. Keep stirring occasionally until the lemon curd thickens. Chill. Ready!

The Italian Meringue Bit

5 egg whites

200g sugar

200ml water

Preparation

In a super clean pan, bring the water & sugar to the boil until it has reached hard ball stage (121 C).

When it reaches 100 C, get the whites whisking on full speed ahead, until soft peaks start to form. Stop!

When the sugar has reached 121 C, start the whisking again and drizzle the syrup over the whites in a slow steady stream.

Continue whisking for 5 to 7 minutes on medium speed until cool and thick.

Pipe over the lemon curd and toast lightly with a blow torch or under the grill.

PB & J

The Peanut Butter Bit

115g soft butter
180g smooth peanut butter
150g icing sugar
1/2 tsp vanilla extract

Preparation

My favourites! If you don't like Reese's Peanut Butter Cups, these aren't for you. Excellent, more for me ...
Top your little cheesecakes with a teaspoon of warmed raspberry jam. Chill. Then top with a spoon of the PB mix and finally drizzle with melted milk chocolate.

- Beat all together until smooth and soft.

PISTACHIO GANACHE & RASPBERRY

150g white chocolate
75ml double cream
1 tsp pistachio purée

Preparation

These require a couple of raspberries dropped into the tart before pouring in your mix. For the topping, you're going to need pistachio purée or if you don't mind the chopped nut texture, just crush up some pistachios and add to the ganache. Top these cheesecakes with the pistachio ganache. While still soft drizzle with a little dark chocolate and top with a pistachio nut.
Mix the chocolate & cream together in a bowl over simmering water until smooth.
Stir in the pistachio purée.

CHOCOLATE BROWNIES

{ These make a big tray. I'd scale it down, but it has tried and tested a thousand times, so I don't want to mess with it! Great for kids parties as an alternative birthday cake - plenty of room to ice a message on top; portioned up, they fit perfectly into a goodie bag; loads of room for candles (especially handy if it's a 40th birthday party) and kids love 'em!
The secret I think, is a nice crust on the outside, yet still nice and fudgy in the middle.
This recipe is for gluten free brownies, which we sell in the shop, but I've substituted the gluten free blend for plain flour before and the recipe is exactly the same (personally, I find the glutenous maximus version slightly better). }

Makes 24

250g soft butter
500g sugar
1 tsp vanilla extract
4 eggs
4 yolks

420g dark chocolate
1 double espresso
60mls boiling water
330g Doves GF flour
1/2 tsp ground sea salt
1 tsp baking powder

Preparation

Pre heat the oven to 180 C.

In a bowl, over simmering water, set the chocolate to melt. When melted, add the espresso and the water (or, just make an espresso measure of fairly strong instant coffee).

Meanwhile, get the butter and sugar creamed together until pale and fluffy.

Slowly start adding the eggs (it may start to look curdled, don't worry, it'll come good).

Fold in the sifted flour, baking powder and salt.

Fold in the chocolate until well mixed.

Spread out into a lined baking tray (mine is 30cm x 42cm - just right to go into a regular oven).

Into the oven, top shelf for 10 mins. Turn the tray around, then 10 more minutes.

(They should have a nice crust and look slightly paler than before they went in).

Leave to cool for several hours - ideally you need to fridge these before portioning up.

180 C 15 - 20 min approx.

GRANOLA FLAPJACKS

{ You can swap and change the types of seeds and dried fruit if you like. Some flapjacks have flour in the recipe, but I always think that they make for a harder flapjack. This one is moist, soft to eat and smells incredible when it's baking! }

Makes 12

300g *butter*

100g *caster sugar*

100g *soft brown sugar*

175ml *honey*

175ml *golden syrup*

400g *jumbo oats*

100g *sultanas*

100g *cranberries*

10 *dried apricots*

10 *dried apples*

4 tbsp *ground almonds*

4 tbsp *seeds (pumpkin & sunflower)*

Preparation

Bowl one: get the sugars, butter, syrup and honey melting together over a pan of simmering water.

Bowl two: stick all the other ingredients in this one!

Mix bowl one and bowl two together. That's it!

Spread into a 9 x 13 inch tin (lined with a sheet of greaseproof paper pressed into it).

Bake in the oven at 170 C fan for 20 to 25 mins approx.

Leave to completely cool before turning out and cutting into portions.

PEAR & ALMOND TART

{ You can change the fruit on this tart if you like, depending upon the season. We've found that peaches, apricots, plums, nectarines, apples and even rhubarb work really well with this recipe.
This is one of the few pastries that works just as well as a sophisticated pudding on an evening as it does with a cup of tea on an afternoon. If serving as a pudding, it's best served slightly warm (about 30 -45 mins after it has come out of the oven) with some fresh homemade custard. }

Takes some mastering, but once you've cracked it, sweet treat options are endless. The trickiest bit is rolling sweet pastry. Ideally, nice and cold but not too hard (as it's very short, and the butter can start to melt over your pin and the worktop, making for a big sticky mess). If it helps, I find that keeping the pastry moving stops it from sticking to the surface - no more than 'two rolls each way' is my mantra! Start by flattening out the pastry by hand into a 2cm thick round. Then on a lightly floured worktop, roll forwards, backwards, forwards and backwards. Stop! Now, give the pastry a quarter turn and repeat until you get the required size. You may need to lightly dust your fingers to get under the pastry to turn and maybe a little on your pin, but go easy with the flour, or you'll dry out the pastry and it will be less pliable and likely to crack.

2 to 3 ripe pears
(peel, quarter and trim out the core)
250g flour
60g sugar
160g unsalted butter
2 yolks
25ml water approx.
pinch of salt

Preparation of the Sweet Pastry

Rub the flour, salt and butter together in a bowl.

Add the yolks and the water and turn out onto the work top.

With a palette knife, bring together to form a dough - do not knead.

Wrap and chill for an hour or so ...

Get yourself a 24cm tart ring on a lined baking sheet and set aside.

On a lightly floured worktop, roll the pastry to an even thickness of a pound coin.

Roll the pastry carefully onto your pin, then loosely drop over the tart ring.

Carefully push the pastry into the edges of the ring, leaving a little pastry overhanging the ring. Don't trim this off yet!

Chill the tart case for an hour.

Line the tart with greaseproof paper and fill with baking beans (we use dried haricot blanc for this).

Bake at 170 C for 30 - 35 mins.

Almond Cream

125g ground almonds

125g soft butter

2 eggs

125g sugar

1/2 tsp almond extract

Preparation

If you have a food processor, get the sugar and butter whizzing around until it's pale and fluffy.

Add the eggs slowly, then pulse in the ground almonds and the extract.

While the almond cream (frangipane) is still soft, spread into the prebaked pastry case.

Arrange the pear quarters on top of the tart and bake at 165 C for 30 minutes approx. The almond cream should have slightly puffed up around the pear pieces and be a lovely golden brown.

Now you can trim the crust off!

For the cheffy touch, we like to finish the tarts by brushing with some warmed apricot jam to give a lovely glaze, then sprinkle with some toasted flaked almonds. Or, simply finish with some icing sugar.

ANDREA'S GINGER CAKE

Andrea is the queen of old fashioned cakes! She's our very own Mrs. Miggins. She's super consistent and a rock in the kitchen. She's also the girl to go to for sweets, old fashioned hard boiled sweets. There's nearly always a bag on the go and I always manage to sniff 'em out.

Andrea tops this cake with lemon icing which is easily made by stirring lemon juice into icing sugar until you have a nice coating consistency. Perfect with a mug o' tea …

Makes 12 portions

300g treacle

300g golden syrup

190g soft brown sugar

225g butter

3 tsp fresh grated ginger

1 1/2 tsp ground ginger

1 1/2 tsp ground cinnamon

375 ml milk

3 eggs

1 1/2 tsp bi-carb (dissolve in 3 tbsp warm water)

450g plain flour

Preparation

Line the tray with grease proof paper and make sure it comes up the sides by about 3 inches.

In a pan on a low heat, melt the butter, treacle, syrup, sugar, ginger and spices together.

In a large bowl, break the eggs and add the milk.

Stir in the melted buttery/sugary mix from the pan and add the bi-carb water.

Finally, stir in the flour. It's going to look strangely loose, but that's ok.

Pour into the lined tin and bake at 170 C for 35 to 45 mins. If it's not cooked after the 'knife test', turn the heat down to 160'c and lay some foil over the cake just to stop it from going too dark before it is ready.

Leave it to cool before taking out and covering with the icing.

CHERRY & ALMOND SLICE

{ They're not cheap, but if you can get those lovely cherries in Kirsch, they're perfect to stud the cake with. After it has been baked, you can drizzle the cake with some of the liquor for a moist, boozy hit! }

Makes 12 portions

250g butter
225g sugar
3 eggs
1 tsp almond extract
225g plain flour

1/ 2 tsp baking powder
150g ground almonds
300g cherry jam
200g pitted fresh cherries

Preparation

Cream the butter and sugar together.
Slowly add the beaten eggs and the almond extract.
Fold in the flour, ground almonds and the baking powder.
In a 9inch by 13inch tray, lined with greaseproof paper, spread half of the mix into the base of the tray.
Carefully, spread the cherry jam onto the cake mix (if it's not a loose set jam, it helps to warm up the jam slightly first).
Finally, spread the rest of the cake mix over the jammy layer.
If you have them, stud the cake all over with the boozy cherries. If not, never mind!
Bake at 170 C for approx. 35 to 40 minutes. (Test with a small knife into the cake - it should come out clean).
Leave to cool, then sprinkle with toasted almonds and icing sugar before portioning.

TARTE TATINS

{ For dinner parties, I prefer to make the traditional large Tarte Tatin, but Saturday mornings we make little individual Tartes (actually, they're not so little – everyone gets a whole apple!).
You'll need a good heavy cast iron or non stick pan that can go on the stove top as well as in the oven.
'Scrap' (trimmings that have been re rolled) puff pastry is better for these I find, you don't want so much puff for these. The trick to these is the caramel. As it's all done in a shallow pan, you can't rely on a sugar thermometer, but don't worry, you don't need one. }

I always have the sink filled with a couple of inches of cold water at the ready – caramel is hard to control, take your eye off it and you'll have plumes of smoke – once you're happy with the colour of the caramel, sit the base of the pan in the water and this will stop the sugar cooking any further.
Another trick is to get the right apples. Some apples turn to mush when they cook, they're too watery.
You need something that can stand a bit of cooking without falling apart. I've found that Cox's, Braeburn and Russets are really good. Definite no nos are Golden Delicious, Granny Smith's and those tasteless American pink apples.

Makes 4

4 good sized Cox's apples
scrap puff or homemade rough
puff

caster sugar
cinnamon sticks
a few knobs of butter

Preparation

Peel the apples and cut them in half from the stalk to the base. Carefully cut out the core and set aside.
Roll out the pastry to about 3mm thick and cut into circles of pastry (about 12cm in diameter).
Heat a good heavy pan (that can also go into the oven) over a medium heat.
Sprinkle caster sugar over the base of the pan and watch as it dissolves in the heat. When it does, start adding more sugar until the pan is a couple of millimetres deep in sugar. As soon as the sugar becomes a golden brown, take off the heat.

Add the apples to the pan, cut side down and cook over a low heat in the caramel with the cinnamon sticks. Space the apples apart in pairs (the second apple needs to ride on top of the first apple), add a couple of knobs of butter to the pan and place the pastry over the apples. Tuck the pastry in over the apples. Ideally, the edge of the pastry needs to be just sitting in the caramel and this will give you nice chewy edges to the pastry once cooked.

Into the oven at 180 C and bake for about 35 minutes. The pastry should be a nice golden colour and crisp. Remove from the oven and leave to cool for about 10 minutes before you attempt to remove them from the pan.

Carefully, with a cranked spatula or a fish slice, get right under the base of the tarts and ease off the caramel base. If they're troublesome to get out, you may need to warm the caramel up a little (either on the stove top or back in the oven for a bit).

Some may leave a bit too much caramel behind in the pan, if so, warm the pan back up and pour the caramel over the apples.

Leave to cool before eating!

PECAN PIE

We've tried a number of American recipes on the counter over the years. Some are surprisingly popular (although there does seem to be a growing American community in the area) and then others, that I think are going to be guaranteed winners, are harder to sell. The pecan pie falls into the surprisingly popular category. But then, why wouldn't it!

Serves 8

150g sugar
100g soaked raisins
90g maple syrup
90g golden syrup
1/2 tsp salt
3 eggs
45g butter
1/2 tsp vanilla
90g pecans

Preparation

Roll out and pre bake a sweet tart case (22 cm x 2 cm deep).
Pre heat the oven to 150 C.
Melt the butter, break up the eggs and mix all the ingredients together.
Pour into the tart shell and bake for roughly 45 to 50 mins.

BLUEBERRY & APPLE COBBLER

You can make this as a tray bake, let it go cold and then cut into squares. Alternatively, in a deeper dish, it makes a great Sunday afternoon pudding. With custard (of course!).

Serves 12

The Shortcake Base And The Cobbler Topping

200g sugar

375g flour

1 tsp baking powder

1/2 tsp salt (check butter)

1 tsp ground cinnamon

200g un-salted butter

1 egg

The Filling

100g sugar

1 tblsp cornflour

250g blueberries

250g apple compote (Bramleys cooked down with some sugar until they are not too sharp)

Preparation

Rub together the sugar, flour, baking powder, salt, cinnamon and butter.

Loosely fold in the beaten egg, but don't form into a dough just yet. Take about two thirds of the mixture and spread over the surface of a lined 33 cm x 23 cm tin.

Lightly press into the tin and chill.

Combine all together - you may not need all the sugar, depending on the blueberries (frozen ones tend to be sweeter I have found).

Spread the fruit mix over the shortcake base.

Finally, scatter the remaining third of the shortcake mix over the surface of the fruit. There won't be enough to cover the whole surface, it's intended to look uneven with patches of fruit showing through the cobbler.

Into the oven, at 175 C for 30 to 40 mins.

HOT CROSS BUNS

{ Another use of the versatile Sweet Bun Dough recipe. Make the dough well ahead of time in the day, then you can chill it to make it more manageable. }

Makes 15

500g strong white flour
10g dried yeast
125g butter – into cubes
70g sugar
1 tsp salt

3 eggs
250g milk
1 tsp vanilla extract
250g soaked raisins
75g mixed peel
2 tsp mixed spice

Preparation

Add the yeast to the milk with a pinch of the sugar and leave to ferment while you weigh out and prepare the rest.

Rub the butter, salt, sugar & flour together with the paddle attachment. When all is mixed in well and resembling fine bread crumbs, switch the paddle for the dough hook.

On a low speed, add the beaten eggs, milk, fruit, peel, spice and vanilla extract.

Mix well for for 5 to 7 mins, cover with cling film and chill.

Line a baking tray (30 cm x 42 cm) with baking parchment.

Remove the dough from the fridge and divide into 15 equal pieces.

Roll into tight balls on a floured surface and space equally into the tray (3 x 5 ideally).

Flour lightly, cover and leave to prove.

Pre heat the oven to 190 C

When doubled in size (they should now be bumping up against each other), prepare your 'cross' mix. There's no recipe for this, it's flour and cold water beaten into a slack paste. It needs to be pipeable, so not too runny. Before you pipe the cross, GENTLY egg wash the buns. Easy does it, or pfffft ... down they go.

Pipe across your buns. If they're in neat rows, hopefully you can just go right across a whole row of buns without stopping.

Bake for 25 mins.

Happy Easter!

PECAN BLONDIES

{ My Sunday treat, if I'm passing by, is a coffee from Bison and a peanut blondie. If I didn't know that they were so calorific, I'd probably get two peanut blondies, but they are and I'm doing my best not to end up like Elvis. I've had a go at numerous recipes to try and recreate these. This recipe is as close as I've got, although I've added pecans to the recipe, partly because I love pecans almost as much as I do peanut butter (I've put some of that in too!) and partly to give it some crunch. }

Makes 12

345g plain flour
1/1/2 tsp baking powder
1 tsp salt
2 tblsp Horlicks
200g soft butter
360g soft brown sugar

2 large eggs
2 tsp vanilla extract
150g chopped pecans
75g golden syrup
75g maple syrup
170g peanut butter

Preparation

Measure out the top four ingredients and run a whisk through them to mix together and to lightly aerate. Set aside.
Cream the butter and sugar together.
Add the eggs, vanilla, the syrups and the peanut butter.
Gradually add the top four ingredients and fold in 75g of the pecans.
Spread out into a lined 33 cm x 23 cm tray and sprinkle with the remaining chopped pecans.
Bake at 170 C for 25 minutes.
Like brownies, you're looking for a crust on top, whilst still fudgey in the centre.
Leave to cool for a couple of hours (ideally, chill before portioning).
These are rich! Small portions will do, served at room temperature with a coffee.

CARAMEL SHORTBREAD

{ One of the few cakes we've had on since the beginning, partly because it's popular and partly because it's dead easy. I think this is originally a Peter Gordon recipe. }

Makes 24 generous portions

3 tins condensed milk
500g butter
300g sugar

300g cornflour
600g plain flour

Preparation

First off, you'll need to boil the cans of condensed milk for 3 hours - don't let the pan boil dry! Always keep the pans simmering under water (Alternatively, you can now buy tins of condensed milk already boiled). Leave to cool completely before opening.

Cream together the butter and sugar until pale, fluffy and soft.

Sift the flours together and fold into the butter and sugar mix.

Take three quarters of the shortbread and press into the base of a greaseproof lined 30cm x 42cm baking tray, then chill.

Remove from the fridge and then scoop out the cooked condensed milk 'caramel'. Spread the caramel over the base of the shortbread. Dip an angled spatula in hot water to help spread the caramel nice and evenly.

With the remaining shortbread mix, sprinkle rough, but small lumps of the shortbread over the caramel.

Into a preheated oven at 160 C for 30 mins. The top should be nice and golden and the caramel just starting to bubble at the edges.

Leave to cool for several hours before cutting into portions.

Occasionally, we use the ganache from the Rocky Road recipe to spread on top of a cooled Caramel Shortbread. I believe it's called 'Millionaire's Shortbread', despite inflation. We just call it Chocolate Caramel Shortbread. Far less capitalist.

DIRTY DONUTS

{ Aside from the salads and some of the soups, there aren't a huge amount of dishes that are going to make you slimmer of the week, but as a once in a while treat, they're fine. Anyway, we only sell these on Saturdays, so even if you wanted to eat them everyday, tough! }

Makes 15

Preparation

From the mother recipe 'sweet bun dough', leave to prove as per recipe, then knock back and roll out to about 2cm thick.

Lightly dust with flour, then with a 3" ring cutter, cut out the donuts - they should weigh 70g - 80g each.

Leave to prove again and when almost doubled in size, turn on the fryer at 180'c. Don't let the donuts fully double up in the prove as they can go pfffft when you pick them up. Leave a little spring in the dough for when they go into the fryer and you'll see them grow before your very eyes in the hot oil.

Carefully drop the donuts into the hot oil. Don't over crowd or your donuts will morph into one big hideous donut. Let them fry on one side for 3 minutes, then carefully flip them over for a further 2 to 3 minutes.

Carefully lift out with a slotted spoon, shake off any excess oil, then onto a paper towel before tossing in caster sugar (if you happen to have made some vanilla sugar with spent pods and are waiting for this sugar that you've made to come into its own, now's the time!).

You can now eat them as they are, but that's not nearly dirty enough. Below are a few of the fillings that we use every Saturday.

To fill, you'll need a piping bag and a wooden spoon. All you need to do is turn your donut on its side, insert the handle of a wooden spoon carefully into the donut, push the end of the spoon in until you can't go anymore and wiggle it about a bit, then pull out. Pipe one of the following into the centre:

Lemon Curd

Follow the recipe for lemon curd in the Little Cheesecake recipe. Just be sure to make the curd a day ahead so that it can chill and be piped.

Crème Brulée

You'll need a sugar thermometer for the brulée bit. In fact, as a crème brulée, it's a bit of a cheat. Crème brulées are usually 'burnt sugar' on the surface of the set custard, but for this recipe, I cook the sugar until it reaches caramel, then quickly remove from the heat. Whilst still liquid, dip the filled donut in the caramel – very carefully! For the filling, you'll need a recipe for crème patissière. You don't have to. I once, on an eggless day at home made some crème pat for donuts by making some extra thick Birds custard. It was good! (don't judge me).

Crème Patissière
500ml milk
1 vanilla pod

100g caster sugar
6 egg yolks
30g flour

Preparation

Heat the milk with the vanilla. Meanwhile beat the yolks, flour and sugar together. Pour a third of the vanilla milk over the yolk, sugar and flour. Mix well, then pour into a pan with the rest of the milk and continue to stir over a low heat until the custard thickens. Leave to chill.

Jam

Don't expect a recipe for jam here. I'm rubbish at it.

Lemon Meringue Pie

Use the lemon curd recipe for the filling and for the top, you'll need to make some Italian meringue and finish with a blow torch.

Banoffee

For the filling, loosely fold whipped cream with mashed banana and a little caramel (tinned Carnation is great for this). For the top, dip in melted chocolate.

MOON PIES

{ The original Moon Pies are a bit like a Wagon Wheel, only more generous on the mallow centre. They're also made by The Chattanooga Bakery, Tennessee which I find exciting in a 1950's Americana kinda way. These have been transformed into a cake and sadly, I haven't found a way of making them round, well not without wasting lots of cut out cake and mallow. }

Makes 24 good ones

This recipe makes a large tray 30 cm x 42 cm, so you'll have to cut them into squares

The Sponge Base	Cream together:	Sieve and fold in:
1/4 cup cocoa	115g unsalted butter – softened	2 1/2 cups plain flour
2 tbsp red food colouring	1 2/3 cups sugar	1 tsp salt
1/4 cup boiling water	add one at a time:	1 tsp bicarbonate of soda
2 cups buttermilk	3 large eggs	
1 tsp vanilla		
1 tbsp cider vinegar		
115g unsalted butter – softened		
1 2/3 cups sugar		
3 large eggs		
2 1/2 cups plain flour		
1 tsp salt		
1 tsp bicarbonate of soda		

Preparation

In a free standing mixer, beat the butter and sugar together until pale and fluffy.

Add the eggs one at a time and then fold in the flour.

In a separate bowl, mix the cocoa, red food colouring, boiling water, buttermilk, vanilla and the cider vinegar. Then fold into the remaining cake mix.

Spread evenly into a 30 x 42cm tin and bake at 170'c for 20 -25 minutes.
Leave to cool, then top with the next layer.

The Jam Layer
Use good quality jam and spread a thin layer over the surface of the sponge.

The Mallow Layer (see method for marshmallows on page 145)
450g sugar
4 1/2 leaves gelatin soaked in 70g water
100g egg whites

Whilst still soft, spread the marshmallow over the layer of jam and allow to set before making the chocolate topping.

Chocolate Layer
250g dark chocolate
125g cream
100g butter
2 tbsp golden syrup

Place all into a bowl set over a pan of simmering water - don't let the bowl touch the water. Mix until smooth and shiny and allow to cool slightly before spreading evenly over the marshmallow.
Allow to set in the fridge and cut into squares using a hot wet knife each time you make a cut into the moon pie.

PARKIN

{ A bonfire night classic ... }

Makes 24

400g self-raising flour
pinch of salt
8 tsp ground ginger
2 tsp ground nutmeg
2 tsp mixed spice
300g oatmeal

700g golden syrup
200g black treacle
400g butter
400g soft brown sugar
4 eggs, beaten
8 dessert spoons milk

Preparation

Preheat oven to 140 C
Sieve together flour, salt, ginger, nutmeg and mixed spice.
Mix in the oatmeal.
Melt down the syrup, treacle, butter and brown sugar and simmer, but don't boil. Then stir in the dry mix and blend together.
Add the beaten egg and milk to the mixture to create a soft, almost pouring, consistency. Pour into a lined 30cm x 42cm tin.
Bake for 1 1/2 hours until firm in the centre.
When cooked, allow to stand for 15 minutes before turning out.
This can then be served.

PAUL'S WHISKY ECCLES CAKES

{ I'm not sure how far removed these are from the original Eccles Cake recipe, but we love 'em. Paul, our moustachioed cake and coffee maker extraordinaire came up with the recipe after discussing our love and obsession with Eccles Cakes. After a tough morning, he would stride into the kitchen and say, "I know what'll cheer us up. How about a T and an E?" and off he'd trot to the bakers down the road and return with 2 hot Eccles cakes and 2 mugs of tea. I miss that guy. }

Makes 12

440g currants

100g melted butter

220g soft brown sugar

2 tsp ground cinnamon

2 tsp mixed spice

2 tbsp whisky (plus more for when baked)

scrap puff pastry

egg whites and caster sugar to glaze

Preparation

Rinse and soak the currants the day before which helps them to swell.

On a low heat, melt the butter, then add everything else (not the pastry!) and stir together. Leave to cool.

Meanwhile, roll out the pastry fairly thin and cut out 24 cm x 5 cm discs.

Egg wash the rims of 12 of the pastry discs and heap spoonfuls of the currant mix into the centre.

Place the other 12 discs on top of the mix. Push the pastry down, squeeze out any air and make sure that the pastry has sealed together. They should now resemble big ravioli.

Fold in the seal of the pastry, so that the excess pastry is now underneath. Put a couple of slashes in the top.

Toss the eccles cakes in egg whites and then in caster sugar and place on a lined baking tray.

At 200 C, bake for 20 - 25 mins. Whilst still hot, drizzle a little whisky into the slashes.

Leave to cool before eating.

PUMPKIN WHOOPIE PIES

Basically, it's 2 damp cookies sandwiched together with a vanilla cream cheese filling. I know that's not really selling it, but they are delicious and full of autumnal-feeling-spices.
A dry bowl, a wet bowl and an old fashioned ice cream scoop is pretty much the key to these (the 'trigger release' kind of scoop that dinner ladies in the eighties used to use to serve up mash. Well, they did at my school anyway).

If you're making your own pumpkin purée (you can use canned), we bake large wedges of the pumpkins under foil until tender, cool, scoop out the flesh from the skin and sit in a sieve and leave in the fridge overnight to catch any extra unneeded moisture.

Makes 16

Dry Bowl	Wet Bowl	Filling
450g plain flour	400g soft brown sugar	500g cream cheese
1 tsp salt	225g vegetable oil	300g icing sugar
1 tsp baking powder	650g pumpkin purée	1 vanilla pod
1 tsp bi carb	2 large eggs	
2 tbsp cinnamon	1 tsp vanilla	
1 tbsp ginger		
1 tbsp ground cloves		

Preparation

Fold the two bowls together and using a wet scoop, scoop something roughly the size of two tablespoons onto lined baking trays. Bake well spaced out - we get four trays of eight from this mix, which makes 16 good sized sandwiches.
10 to 12 minutes at 175 C. Make the filling by beating together the cream cheese, icing sugar and seeds from the vanilla pod.
Leave to cool before sandwiching together with sweetened cream cheese.

STICKY TOFFEE CAKE

85g butter (plus extra for
greasing the tin)
145g caster sugar
1 tsp vanilla essence
3 eggs
175g self raising flour
150ml boiling water
1 shot of espresso
1 tsp bicarbonate of soda
175g pitted dates

Preparation

Put dates into a bowl, cover with the boiling water, vanilla, coffee and bi-carb and leave to soak over night. Blend until smooth.

Line a 9 inch x 13 inch bread tin with butter taking care to make sure there is a good all over covering.

Cream together the butter and sugar. Make sure to mix well to a light and fluffy consistency.

Sift the flour.

Beat the eggs and add them to the butter mix one at a time, should the mix look like it will split add a spoonful of the flour.

Add the flour to the butter mix.

Fold date purée into the butter mix, taking care not to knock too much air out of the mix.

45 - 55 mins at 160 C.

SALTED CARAMEL TOFFEE SAUCE

200g caster sugar
100g butter – salted
150ml double cream
1 tsp salt

Preparation

Heat the sugar in a heavy pan - on a low heat to start and watch as it dissolves and slowly turns to a light caramel colour.

With a wooden spoon, carefully stir in the cream - watch out, it will bubble violently! Keep the pan on a simmer and keep stirring until completely smooth.

Stir in the butter until it is completely melted.

Add the salt and remove from the heat.

To eat, we like to pour some of the sauce over the cake, cover in foil and bake for 10 - 12 minutes until the sauce has dissolved into the cake, leave to cool slightly, transfer to a cake stand.

Warm some of the caramel sauce and drizzle over the cake.

CHEEKY RASCALS

{ Just like making scones. I now drop the lard to keep 'em veggie, but here's the original recipe. }

Makes 6

450g flour
15g baking powder
100g sugar
45g butter
45g lard (or butter if veggie)
100g mixed fruit (raisins,
currants, chopped mixed peel)

2 eggs
100ml milk – approx.
1 tsp vanilla
1 tsp mixed spice
12 plump glacé cherries
24 whole blanched almonds
egg wash

Preparation

Sift the flour and baking powder together.
Add the butter, lard and sugar and rub together until fine.
Stir in the fruit and the spices, then add the beaten egg, milk and vanilla. Mix loosely on a floured table top and pat into a round of 1.5 cm deep.
Using a 9 cm cutter, cut out six rascals and place onto a lined tray.
Egg wash each, then push in the cherries (for eyes) and the whole almonds (for handsome teeth).
180 C 20 - 25 mins.

FRUIT N' SPICE LOAF

{ I love this bread, particularly toasted, although it can be a nightmare to toast as it goes from 'not quite ready' to 'fruit loaf inferno' in about 10 seconds. Delicious hot, toasted and buttered. }

375g strong white flour
1 tsp salt
7g yeast
1 tsp mixed spice
1 tsp cinnamon
1 tsp grated nutmeg
1 orange – zest only

50g caster sugar
50g diced butter
150ml milk
1 egg
50g mixed peel
100g mix of currants, sultanas and raisins

Preparation

Rub the butter into the flour and salt until fine.

Add the fruit, zest and spices.

Add the beaten egg, yeast, milk and knead until smooth and elastic for about 5 mins.

Leave to prove, covered in cling film until doubled in size.

Divide the dough into two equal amounts, shape and place into two lightly oiled bread tins (500g tins).

Cover and leave to prove until doubled.

Into a pre heated oven at 180 C for 30 mins.

Turn out of the tins and leave to cool on a rack.

ICE CREAM SANDWICH

{
We've tried lots of different cookies and biscuits over the years, but whenever making them with the kids, this is the recipe we always use. Ideally, you want your cookies crisp around the edges and chewy in the centre. Divide and measure the cookie dough into 50g lumps, then roll into balls. As they spread out and bake around the edges in the oven, the centre is only just beginning to cook. Chewy!
}

Makes 40 to 50 cookies

Choc chip cookies
400g dark choc chips
500g butter
400g sugar
300g brown sugar

4 eggs
2 tsp vanilla
600g flour
2 tsp baking powder
pinch of salt

Preparation

Beat soft butter and sugars together with vanilla.

Add the eggs.

Fold in the sifted flour, salt and baking powder, then add the chocolate.

Allow to cool, then divide into 50g pieces and roll into a ball. Chill.

Bake at 175 C for 8 to 10 mins. Leave to cool on a rack.

Take one of the cookies and heap some good quality ice cream into the centre of the cookie (if you have a particularly large jaw, put plenty of ice cream in the cookies), then pop the other cookie on top. Ready! However, at this stage, you can wrap the ice cream sandwiches in foil and pop back in the freezer until the BBQ is over, then hand out your little foil parcels of frozen awesomeness (I actually prefer them like this - the ice cream and the cookies bond together better - plus I kinda like that slightly soggy centre to the cookie after it has been pressed against the ice cream over night).

PEACH & PISTACHIO PUFFS

{ If you have ready made puff pastry and some frangipane left over from another recipe (it keeps well in the fridge), these are really easy to knock up. The pistachio purée isn't easy to find, so you can either leave it out of the recipe or come and borrow some from me ... }

Makes 4

300g puff pastry
4 fresh ripe peaches
6 tbsp of Frangipane – recipe below
50g apricot jam + 25g water
1 egg yolk and a little milk for egg wash
a couple of teaspoons of broken pistachios

Preparation

Roll the puff pastry out to about 5mm thick. Cut out 6inch x 4inch x 4inch squares and set onto a lined baking tray.

Egg wash the edges of the pastry and then prick the centre of the pastry squares with a fork.

Spoon a heap of the frangipane in the centre of each pastry, then top with peach halves (that's if they will cut into half - sometimes they'll cling to the stone for dear life, even if they are really ripe - in this case, slices of peach is fine).

Bake at 180 C for 25 mins approx. until the pastry is crisp (particularly in the centre as this takes a little longer).

Simmer the apricot jam and water together, then brush the peaches with the glaze and sprinkle with the broken pistachios.

Frangipane

125g butter
125g sugar

Cream together, then beat in ...

2 eggs

Then fold in a little of each into the butter and sugar mix:

30g flour
125g ground almonds
1 tsp almond extract or a little amaretto
1 tsp pistachio paste

Chill before use.

PEANUT BUTTER BROWNIES

{All we've done here is taken our brownie recipe, baked it as usual and then spread with a good layer of peanut butter frosting.

Here's the recipe again for the brownies ...

Makes 24

250g soft butter
500g sugar
1 tsp vanilla
4 eggs
4 yolks
420g dark chocolate

1 double espresso
60mls boiling water
330g Doves GF flour
1/2 tsp ground sea salt
1 tsp baking powder

Preparation

Pre heat the oven to 180 C.

Set the chocolate to melt in a bowl over simmering water. When melted, add the espresso and the water (or just make an espresso measure of fairly strong instant coffee).

Meanwhile, get the butter and sugar creamed together until pale and fluffy.

Slowly start adding the eggs (it may start to look curdled, don't worry, it'll come good).

Fold in the sifted flour, baking powder and salt.

Fold in the chocolate until well mixed.

Spread out into a lined baking tray (mine is 30cm x 42cm - just big small enough to go into a regular oven).

Into the oven, top shelf for 10 mins. Turn the tray around, then 10 more minutes.

They should have a nice crust and look slightly paler than before they went in.

And then finish with a good layer of this before portioning.

Peanut Butter Frosting

230g butter
365g peanut butter
300g icing sugar
1/2 tsp vanilla extract

Preparation

In a free standing mixer add the soft (not melted) butter, peanut butter, icing sugar and vanilla with the paddle beater attachment.
Cover the bowl with a tea towel to prevent yourself getting consumed in a cloud of icing sugar. Start the machine off slow to begin, then gradually increase the speed. Once the brownie is completely cool spread the surface of the brownie with peanut butter frosting.

LEMON DRIZZLE CAKE

When we first opened, this was one of only a (small) hatful of sweet recipes that I knew. I'd bake two everyday that would be ready by lunchtime and within an hour, they'd usually be gone.
If hot syrup is poured over hot cake, the drizzle will get through more, making for a really zingy and moist cake. They're also best eaten on the same day.

Makes a 1lb loaf tin

125g butter – soft
175g sugar
2 large eggs
1 lemon – zested
175g self raising flour
pinch 'o' salt
4 tsp milk

Drizzle
Juice of 1 1/2 lemons
100g icing sugar

Preparation

Cream the butter, zest and sugar together.
Beat in the eggs and then carefully fold in the sifted flour and salt.
Finally add the milk and pour/dollop the mix into a 1lb loaf tin that has been lined on the base with a strip of greaseproof paper.
Bake at 170 C fan for 30 to 40 minutes - the cake is ready when a small knife is inserted into the centre of the cake and comes out clean.

Preparation of the Drizzle

Simmer the two together and pour over the cake while both are still hot.

BLUEBERRY SCONES

In the café we get 12 big scones from this recipe, but you could quite easily get 24 good sized afternoon tea ones out of this batch.

These make for a really moist scone, as it's quite a wet mix and because of this, they also keep really well. (If there are ever any left at the shop, we bring them home and the kids have them in their packed lunches!).

Pre heat the oven 190 C fan/200 C

900g plain flour - sifted

45g baking powder – sifted with the flour

180g unsalted butter – diced into 1cm chunks

200g caster sugar

250g frozen or fresh blueberries

550ml milk

1 tsp vanilla extract – mix into the milk

Preparation of the dough

In a free standing mixer with the paddle attachment, begin rubbing the dry ingredients together with the butter until the butter is well mixed in (should resemble fine breadcrumbs at this stage).

Add the blueberries and mix in lightly.

Preparation

Mix the vanilla into the milk, then add the milk and vanilla to the dry mix - if using a mixer, just a few turns of the paddle will do - you don't want to end up with tough scones.

Turn out onto a floured table, divide into two equal lumps of scone dough.

Shape each piece of dough into a 3cm deep round of dough.

Cut each round of dough into 6 even wedges.

Place the scones onto a tray lined with greaseproof paper, and brush the tops with egg yolk.

Into the oven for 20 - 25 mins, depending upon the size you have made the scones. You can always test the scones at this point by tapping them on the bottom! (Listen out for a fairly hollow sound).

"I wish I could chop things like a chef"

"Have you got a decent knife?"

"No"

"If this book sells I'll give you this one!"